FALLING IN LOVE WITH GOD

Reflections on Prayer

Dr. J. Alfred Smith, Sr.

BIBLE STUDY APPLICATIONS

Colleen Birchett, Ph.D.

Urban Ministries, Inc.
The African American Christian Publishing
& Communications Co.

Urban Ministries, Inc.
Chicago, Illinois

Publisher
Urban Ministries, Inc.
P.O. Box 436987
Chicago, IL 60643-6987
1.800.860.8642

First Edition
Second Printing 1998
ISBN: 0-940955-36-9
Catalog No. 10-6302

DEDICATION

This book is dedicated in love to my wife JoAnna, my children, grandchildren, great-grandchildren, and to all persons who strive to love mercy, do justly, and walk humbly with God. It is also dedicated to all the students who have studied in spirituality courses under me at American Baptist Seminary of the West and Fuller Theological Seminary.

Dr. J. Alfred Smith, Sr.

ACKNOWLEDGMENTS

I live in a home with a praying wife who awakens me every morning with her voice lifted up in song and prayer. Her prayers are the first sounds heard in our house. She usually concludes her prayer period with devotional Bible study that is followed with a breakfast of toast and coffee. JoAnna Smith walks daily with God. Her example encouraged me to write this book.

I am deeply indebted to a number of persons for their very large help in producing this book. I deeply appreciate the editorial efforts of the Reverend Jini Kilgore Ross. She used her editorial creativity in making the first draft of changes that were needed in the manuscript.

I am so grateful to my son and Co-Pastor, Reverend J. Alfred Smith, Jr., the Pastoral Staff, and the Prayer Ministry Team for their support.

Ms. Marjie H. Lawson worked hard in typing and proofreading the manuscript again and again, and in locating the proper citations for footnotes. To her, I am grateful.

I must thank Dr. Colleen Birchett for her biblical and spiritual insights. To Urban Ministries and Dr. Melvin Banks, I give special thanks for his wise counsel and guidance and for publishing this book.

Prayerfully,

Dr. J. Alfred Smith, Sr.

TABLE OF CONTENTS

PREFACE

Mortimer Arias, the South American theologian and churchman, cautions that the fatal mistake made by the first generation of Christians is about to be repeated in far too many quarters at the end of the 20th century by this present generation of Christians. Jesus commanded His followers to "make disciples," and they did—in Jerusalem, in all of Judea, in Samaria, and all over North Africa, and then Europe. Many of them, however, made a critical mistake. They did not "make disciples" in their own homes!

They did not evangelize their own children. They did not teach them to observe whatever the Lord had commanded them. They did not teach their own children the spiritual disciplines that the Lord observed and practiced daily, and, as a result, the next generation of Christians was sidetracked into arguments, discussions, debates, and schismatic fights over gnosticism, Manichaeism, Arianism, and docetism.

Because they were not imitating and emulating the life that Jesus lived, they got off track and ended up making doctrine instead of making disciples. Jesus lived a life of prayer, and making disciples means (in part) teaching would-be followers the importance of prayer, the discipline of prayer, the mechanics of prayer, the dynamics of prayer, and the practice of prayer.

Pastor Harry Blake of Shreveport, Louisiana, reminds us that the only thing Jesus ever did all night long was pray! Jesus lived a life of prayer. His every action, His every decision, and all of His miracles were bathed in prayer. Before He chose His disciples, He prayed. Before He fed the 5,000, He prayed. Before He raised Lazarus from the dead, He prayed. He had a private praying place in the Garden of Gethsemane. That is how Judas knew where to find Him!

When the 12 who were closest to Him wanted to tap into the secret of divine power, they did not ask the Lord to teach them how to raise the dead or teach them how to turn a few fish and loaves into enough groceries to feed thousands of people. What they asked Him to do was teach them how to pray! They knew that prayer was the key; and they wanted access to that power that came straight from God.

Arias maintains that because the disciples did not make disciples of those right behind them by teaching them how to pray, their children made doctrinal and heretical mistakes that are being repeated in the 1990s and that continue to have negative implications for the Church of Jesus Christ as it faces the 21st century. So many churches have praise teams and awesome choirs, lively worship and Holy Ghost-filled Sunday services, but the members have not been made disciples! They have not been taught the discipline of prayer.

So many churches—even the megachurches—have two to six thousand worshipers on a Sunday morning and less than 100 people in their prayer services. So many church boards, committees, and organizations rush through the opening and closing prayer periods that it seems like prayer is just a perfunctory chore that makes the proceedings authentically Christian. The 20th century disciples of Jesus have not been taught the discipline of prayer. As a result, we have made members, but not disciples!

Dr. J. Alfred Smith, Sr., is a pastor after God's own heart, and his burning desire to move a new generation of Allen Temple's members from membership to discipleship through this particular spiritual exercise is evident in the following pages. His insights are challenging. His methodology is remarkably replicable, and the results have been phenomenal. It is my prayer that every Christian who picks up this volume will learn not just the theory which undergirds this congregation's revival, but will also learn the practice of prayer which undergirds our every moment!

Dr. Jeremiah A. Wright, Jr.
Trinity United Church of Christ
Chicago, Illinois

FOREWORD

The Allen Temple Baptist Church family has numerous awards and citations for performing effective urban church ministry. The outreach programs touch every facet of human life from the womb to the tomb. The Healthy Start Program provides pre-natal care, post-natal care, classes in parenting, and counseling for families and for individuals. There is even an Allen Temple Federal Credit Union with assets well over $6,000,000. There are seminars on managing finances in these changing times and on investments and community economic development. A Job Information Center assists in solving the problems of unemployment and underemployment.

The Allen Temple Haight Ashbury Drug and Alcohol Recovery Center assists recovering addicts and alcoholics. Treatment is given by physicians, nurses, counselors, and the clergy. The Prison Ministry assists prisoners and their families. Ex-offenders are clothed, counseled, and given comfort and assistance in obtaining housing and employment.

Allen Temple's overseas mission work sponsors a church, clinic and school in Sierra Leone, West Africa, provides support for International Missions of The American Baptist Churches, U.S.A., and the overseas missions of The Progressive National Baptist Convention, Inc. An AIDS Hospice Ministry and two housing complexes for the elderly are a part of the ministries of Allen Temple Baptist Church. In late 1995 funding was received from HUD for an additional 50 units of senior housing and 25 units of housing for those living with the HIV/AIDS virus. The AIDS housing complex will be the first in the nation to be built by a Black church. Interface Institute, an after-school tutorial program, provides educational enrichment in mathematics, science, English, and computer literacy for students in seventh, eighth and ninth grades. A scholarship fund is available to help college and seminary students pay for their education.

The church is noted for training many lay ministers and volunteers to work with a pastoral staff of eight ordained clergy, who visit the sick and shut-in at home and in hospitals, conduct street ministries and provide grief counseling. A cancer support group provides comfort and spiritual support to individuals and their families. Because of this activism, spiritual burnout and the fatigue of failure made it necessary for the church to strengthen her spiritual roots through prayer and discipleship.

This book endeavors to describe the fruitful efforts of Allen Temple Baptist Church in deepening the spirituality of the church through prayer and discipleship. Under the leadership of the senior pastor, the church is promoting among the laity the following disciplines:

1. The discipline of devotion, which requires daily prayer and Scripture reading.

2. The discipline of study, which requires participation in spiritual development classes for new church members; a men's discipleship class; children, youth, and young adult Bible classes; Women's Mission classes; leadership development seminars; and classes on Baptist doctrine taught by the Senior Pastor. There is Thursday evening prayer and Bible study along with 25 weekly Home Bible Study classes in the East Bay counties of Alameda and Contra Costa.

3. The discipline of evangelism, which involves recruiting and training per sons for friendship evangelism, lifestyle evangelism in the areas of Public Mission and Social Justice, as well as street preaching and door-to-door evangelism. With the help of the prayer warriors who meet each Tuesday at noon, persons are spiritually prepared to share unapologetically the good news of Jesus Christ to the nonchurched.

4. The discipline of worship includes three services on Sundays. The largest service is at 8:00 a.m. The second service is at 11:15 a.m. The third service is at 5:30 p.m., and is conducted by the Hispanic minister on staff. This Spanish speaking service, as well as church school, is well attended and is supported by bilingual African American members who are committed to reconciling action with the growing Hispanic population in Oakland.

5. The discipline of prayer involves the total membership in the recruiting of lay persons of every age grouping to lead the Thursday evening prayer services from 7:00 p.m. to 8:00 p.m. Following the prayer services, the Senior Pastor and other co-teachers lead Bible studies that emphasize prayer, discipleship, and evangelism. Seventy-five percent of the preaching by the pastoral staff during 1993 was a thematic development of prayer. The discipline of prayer also involves the total membership in a January Prayer Revival.

Dr. J. Alfred Smith, Sr.
Senior Pastor
Allen Temple Baptist Church
Oakland, California 94621

A BRIEF AUTOBIOGRAPHY

Falling in Love with God started in my early childhood. It is a romance that continues to this day. At times, due to my own human fragility, there have been lapses in the romance. However, I find that I am at my best as a human being when I am faithful in my daily walk with God. Hence, it is my desire to not be simply an effective, well-trained teacher, preacher, and pastor, but one who genuinely loves mercy, does justly, and walks humbly with God. Permit me to share with you a glimpse of my own prayer pilgrimage.

As early as I can remember, my childhood days during the era of the Depression were baptized in a home environment of prayer and worship. The mother of my mother, who was born in the Mississippi Delta, awakened me and my younger brother Joseph, each morning by singing: "I woke up this morning with my mind stayed on Jesus." In a small four-room house in Kansas City, Missouri, the voice of Grandmother Martha was often blended with the voice of my mother's sister, Aunt Louise. This aunt, who was the community soloist at funerals, would often rehearse for singing engagements by singing the gospel music of Thomas A. Dorsey. She would use as her musical textbook, *The Gospel Pearls,* which contained gospels, spirituals, and hymns.

Very passionately, sometimes with tears, the melodious voice of my mother Amy would vibrate with great intensity as she pleaded with God for wisdom in rearing two sons as a single parent. She asked God to give her physical strength to earn her a meager income as a domestic doing day work of washing, ironing, and cleaning in the homes of prosperous white families in racially segregated Kansas City, Missouri. Grandmother Martha left the "Egypt land" of Mississippi looking for the "promised land" of Chicago, but her funds were depleted. So she settled in Kansas City with her children: Mother Amy, Aunt Louise, and Uncle Charley. Without an adult male presence to help them in their exodus from Jamestown, Mississippi, God was their invisible means of support. Aunt Louise married Uncle Percy in Kansas

City, and he became the lone male tower of strength in our family, until he became disabled while working as a stevedore for the Missouri Pacific Railroad. I never heard Uncle Percy pray until the evening years of his life, when I had become an adult.

Saturday was a busy day for Joseph and me. We had to read and recite the Sunday School lesson in the presence of Grandmother Martha. She corrected our mistakes and then she commanded us to shine our Sunday shoes and to present her with our Sunday clothes so she could iron them. When we became older, we did the ironing.

Early Sunday morning we would arise and prepare for the long walk to the Pilgrim Rest Baptist Church at 35th and Hardesty. We were required to attend 9:00 a.m. Sunday School, 11:00 a.m. morning worship, Baptist Young Peoples' Union at 6:00 p.m. and the evening worship at 7:00 p.m. On Sunday afternoons the pastor or the visiting guest preacher would be invited to our home for Sunday dinner. This was a special event when our best dishes were used and we had to be on our best behavior. Apart from the formal aspects of church attendance was a separate awareness of prayer being as normal in our daily living as eating, sleeping, and breathing.

In my private moments, I would often sit under an elm tree and experience the wonder and amazement of my existence within the mystery of the created universe. My childhood mind had hundreds of unanswered questions about the marvels of nature and the meaning of my own life. Even though this questioning was a form of prayer in that I was asking God to supply me with answers and with a view of God's presence, I never ceased living in awe of the mystery of God and creation. The fluffy white clouds suspended between the blue sky above and the earth below; the symphony of sounds of singing birds and the rhythmic rustling of leaves responding to the cadence of the wind, all moved me to marvel at the creative imagination of the invisible one called God. I observed the blushing sunset of evening and the rich colors of the rainbow after a summer rain, and with the intuition of a child, I know that a hidden, invisible power whom we call God was the originating and sustaining Creator of life as I was experiencing it. I can remember rising up very early on school days just to run out of doors to see which new birth and blossoming was taking place on the willow trees growing on the side of our house. As a child I thought it strange that I could not see this God with my naked eye, but I could see the work of this God in the beautiful, diverse fields and flowers.

This God whom I could not see was always present. At any time my grandmother would spontaneously say, "Lord, have mercy" or "Thank You, Jesus." Because Grandmother and Mother talked to God in an audible fashion, I never doubted the reality of the God I could not see, because I loved and trusted them and I knew they were sane.

In fact, I saw the answer to their prayers. An angry tornado hit our poor neighborhood of tar paper shacks called houses. Many of the houses rested on a foundation of weak concrete blocks. When the wind was at its worst, objects flew past our windows. Trees were uprooted, our house raised up off its foundation. While brother Joseph and I hid under the dining room table ready for the old house to fly away like a bird, we could hear Grandmother Martha say: "Lord, please save us." In fear brother Joseph prayed as never before. I heard him say: "Lord, Grandmother said please." No sooner than his words were spoken, the house rested on its foundation. The next day we could see devastation all around us. Lives were lost. But we were spared. No critical thinker, no logician, no philosopher will ever convince us that God did not choose to save us. Theologians may argue that it does violence to the moral nature of God to say that God answered our prayers while others were not so fortunate as to have their prayers answered. I only know that God chose to save us in a situation that was life threatening. I only know that whatever our outcome could have been, we chose to face life or death with prayer. I only know that Grandmother prayed to this God as if this God knew her and cared for her and her family.

As a ten-year-old boy who almost drowned in the river at a camp for Cub Scouts and Boy Scouts, I remember seeing every event of my short life pass before me after I had gone down under the water for the third time. I am convinced now as I was then that the God of Martha, Amy, and Louise heard their prayers and sent a stranger into the river to pull me to safety. Later on this person became Coach Mayfield, who trained me to play defensive and offensive line on the Coles High School football team.

Upon accepting Jesus Christ as my personal Saviour, Grandmother Martha and Mother Amy said to me: "James, we are going to leave you alone on this earth someday. We don't have money to leave you. So we are going to teach you and young Joseph to pray." Both my brother and I are grateful for these women tutoring our tongues to communicate with God, whom we had known intuitively in our earliest childhood experiences.

During the rough years of childhood our mother became sick unto death.

Having no hospital insurance, Mama Amy was attended to by missionary women of the church and by Grandmother Martha, Aunt Louise, and close friends. A time of crisis had come. People spoke in hushed voices. My brother and I were called in to see our mother alive for the last time. She was not coherent or clear in her speaking. But after she told me to care for my younger brother, Joseph, we were led out of the small bedroom. The missionary sisters prayed all night. Dr. Thomas Jones, our family doctor from Meharry Medical School in Nashville, worked with Mother. The next morning, Mama Amy was out of danger. God blessed us to have our mother until her 89th year.

The wonder of prayer has nourished my faith far beyond the horizon of my critical thinking about systematic and philosophical theology. I have been blessed to study in some of the respected institutions of higher education. I strive to follow a continuing education plan that will enable me to have a growing faith that is intellectually respectable. My training has helped me to learn that problems can be solved with intellectual know-how. But mystery lives beyond the horizon of reason in the arena where only God is sovereign and ultimate. Prayer empowers me to live by faith, and prayer enables me to get up off the ground of defeat when life strikes with cruel blows.

Prayer for me is not pressure to get God to do my bidding. Prayer is my romance with God. Prayer makes me aware of God's presence. Prayer makes me aware of God's closeness, as the one who is always working to create viable options for me to choose in the struggle to have the courage to triumph in the presence of the ills and evils which threaten my existence. No matter what transpires, God is sovereign. This God is Emmanuel who is with us in pathos and pleasure and in tribulation and triumph. I never confuse the silence of God with the absence of God. God is most present in silence because God has discretionary power. Were it not for the discretionary power of God, you and I in the limitations of our intelligence, would pray prayers that would destroy us were the requests granted. In our love affair with God, prayer is always full surrender to the ultimate will of God. Prayer enables us to trust God fully with the mystery of life and death.

A prayerful romance with God joins us in embracing the mood and mind of Jesus. You and I will allow our hearts to be broken by the things which break the heart of God. Evil in all of its forms hurts God. The poverty of those poor in soul, the pain of the oppressed, the predicament of prisoners of addiction, the meanness of the mighty, the mediocrity of the masses, and the scandal of apathy in the church as the church recoils from challenging evil, are things which break God's heart. Prayer links us with God in the work of helping to clean up a dirty world, and in touching the ugliness of the individual with the beauty of Jesus Christ. In our romance with God, each of us is called to a disciplined life of righteousness, and a daily walk of loving mercy, doing justly, and walking humbly with God. May this book, along with the leader's guide, be of assistance in teaching the reader to love God with the whole heart.

INTRODUCTION

In *Falling in Love with God: Reflections on Prayer,* Dr. J. Alfred Smith, Sr. presents guidelines for establishing intimacy with God. He makes the point that Christians must be people of prayer. He cites many examples of how far prayer can take us, noting that an intimate relationship with God, established through prayer, helps one to "make it" through the most difficult of life's circumstances. African American history is filled with people who are witnesses to that fact. History contains a great "cloud of African American witnesses" who prayed through the most difficult of circumstances, and whose prayers carried them on to victory over extreme adversity. Richard Allen, Sojourner Truth and Thomas Dorsey are three examples of African Americans who prayed their way through adversity. Dr. Smith poses the question, "How far will your prayers take you?" One way to explore an answer to that question is to consider the lives of these three "giants."

Upon completion of this introduction, hopefully you, the reader, will be enticed to study very carefully the principles presented by Dr. J. Alfred Smith, Sr., pastor of Allen Temple Baptist Church, in an effort to develop intimacy with God—the type of intimacy that is similar to "falling in love." Hopefully, upon completion of the book itself you will be motivated to seek a closer relationship with God by practicing the principles laid down by Dr. Smith in this book. Then, hopefully, you will have the type of energy that will allow you to meet the many challenges that life will present, as you and the African American community march toward and into the 21st century.

The lives of Richard Allen, Sojourner Truth and Thomas Dorsey have been studied from many vantage points. However, few studies have examined the prayers they prayed in the midst of their struggles.

Richard Allen. The year was 1786, ten years after the Revolutionary War ended in 1776. The place was Philadelphia, the predominantly white St. George's Methodist Episcopal Church. Richard Allen, Absalom Jones and William White had just been pulled from their feet by the white deacons of the church as they were praying. Why? They were praying in the "whites only" section. In protest, all the Black members of the church walked out. It didn't make any sense. What "was" and what should have been were completely "out of sync."

Richard Allen had been phenomenally successful in adding hundreds of Black members to that church. There were so many new people that he was asked by the white Methodist elder in charge to hold separate prayer meetings for Black people, at 5:00 a.m. That hadn't made any sense. Therefore, Allen proposed building a separate place of worship. When some of the white members rejected that proposal, he and some of the other Black men of the church were allowed to build an addition to the church to create more space for people to sit.

No doubt, Richard Allen wondered how people who claimed to uphold the Bible could also uphold segregated Sabbaths. It must have seemed absurd. However, this was not the first or the last of the absurdities that had an impact on Allen's life. Probably he considered it absurd that he had to ask the permission of his slave master to join the Methodist Society in the first place. It must also have seemed absurd that the same master who considered himself to be a Christian, would require Allen to raise $2,000 from odd jobs to purchase Allen's family's freedom.[1]

Allen lived in an era when 236,400 out of 325,806 Black people in this country were held in bondage.[2] That is, at least three out of every four Black people held the status of slaves. To Allen and other free African Americans at the time, slavery didn't make any sense, considering the important role that Black people had played in the Revolutionary War. When the war started, Richard Allen was 16 years old. He had worked as a wagon driver during the war. He must have thought it strange that people such as Patrick Henry, who cried out rhetoric such as, "Give me liberty or give me death!" did not apply the same rhetoric to Black people.

Allen must have heard about Crispus Attucks, a runaway slave, who was the first to die in the Boston Massacre which directly led to the outburst of the Revolutionary War. He must have known about the Black soldiers who rode with Paul Revere.[3] However, what might have seemed puzzling to him and to so many other Black people at the time was why, in light of how many Black people had already participated in the war, General George Washington did not, at first, approve of Black soldiers fighting in the Continental Army. Why was it that Washington only changed his mind when the British army began to recruit Black soldiers, both runaway slaves and free men? Again, what was and what should have been were completely "out of sync."[4]

By 1778, even though over 3,000 Black soldiers had fought in the war,[5] and even though Black soldiers such as Prince Whipple had served as Washington's bodyguards, protecting him during numerous battles, and even though Black soldiers such as Pompey were given public honors for bravery,[6] still General Washington maintained segregated troops and forbade the recruitment of Black men other than free ones.[7] Probably all of this baffled Richard Allen.

Probably Allen realized that regardless of what Black people did, the rhetoric of the Revolutionary War would not be applied to them. All during the time they were helping to free the American colonies from British domination, colonies throughout the country were passing laws to restrict the freedom of Black people. In 1777, North Carolina reenacted a colonial law that prohibited slave owners from allowing slaves to purchase their freedom, or from manumitting them in any other way.[8]

In 1778, 300 former slaves held off 1,500 British troops, but in that same year, Massachusetts passed a law prohibiting free African Americans from voting.[9] In 1780, although two Black people aided in capturing a British spy, in that same year, Maryland became the only southern state to authorize slaves to enlist in the military.[10] Two years later, in 1782, Virginia passed a law allowing slave owners to manumit Blacks, but denying free Black people the right to vote.[11]

By 1783, 10,000 Black people had fought in the Continental Armies, with 5,000 as regular soldiers.[12] Still, in 1783, Maryland passed a law prohibiting free Black people from voting.[13] Even though Phoebe Frances, a Black servant, had exposed a plot of a Thomas Hubey to overthrow General George Washington and restore the country to British rule, for the most part, the status of African Americans remained unchanged.[14] When the war was over and the Constitution of the United States was written, the importation of African slaves for another 21 years was approved,[15] and voting power of representatives of slave owners was determined by counting Black people as three-fifths of a person each.[16]

Richard Allen would have been 28 years old when the law prohibiting the further importation of African slaves went into effect, in 1808. He would have been aware that plantation owners were now breeding Black women with Black men serving as studs, and dismembering Black families to supply the cotton plantations with home-grown slaves. Allen lived in the era of slave auctions, of slaves being transported over land with their ankles chained together, and of as many as 25% of them dying along the way. He lived in the era when African slaves were illegally smuggled into the country in horrible conditions and sold to plantation owners.

Allen was keenly aware that free Black people who attended white churches were still confined to a particular section of the church, usually the balcony. Therefore, when he and his companions were dragged from their feet while praying in a church that they had helped to build, this incident was just one of a long list of absurdities with which he had to deal. Somewhere in the midst of it all, he prayed:

"I believe, Oh God, that Thou art an eternal, incompressible spirit, infinite in all perfection; who didst make all things out of nothing, and dost govern them all by Thy wise providence. Let me always adore Thee with profound humility, as my Sovereign Lord; and help me to love and praise Thee with godlike affections and suitable devotion."[17]

This was a man who must have had an intimate relationship with God. How far did his prayers take him? Richard Allen went on to build one independent Black church after another, and eventually these churches became the African Methodist Episcopal Church denomination, which now has nearly three million members.

Sojourner Truth. Sojourner Truth was another historic Black figure who, in spite of cruel circumstances, fell in love with God, through prayer. The year was 1826. The place was New Paltz, New York. "Belle," or Sojourner Truth had just discovered that her former slave owner, Mr. Dumont, was responsible for her son being sold to Alabama. As she sat by the side of the road, holding her head between her worn, trembling hands, she did not understand what to do.[18] This was the last in a series of encounters with Dumont that did not make sense.

New York State law prohibited selling any slave outside of the state, and all minors were to be set free at 21 years of age. Moreover, on Freedom Day, just two years away, all of the slaves in New York State were to be set free.[19] Dumont had promised Belle that he would free her one year ahead of time. But he had changed his mind, causing her to run away to the home of Isaac Van Wagenen and his wife Maria, who later purchased her freedom.

She had endured all of that, only to discover that her former master Dumont had told yet another lie. He had promised her that he would never allow her five-year-old son to leave the state. However, Dumont sold him to a Dr. Gedney who took him as far as New York City and then sold him to his brother, Solomon Gedney. Solomon Gedney sold her son to a wealthy planter by the name of Fowler, who lived in Alabama, a cotton-producing state. The entire transaction was illegal. She could not believe that Dumont, a supposedly Christian man, had both lied and violated the law, when he had taught her never to lie to him and never to break the law.

In her grief, possibly Sojourner Truth could not see that what had happened to her family was a part of a much larger cruel system of the domestic slave trade. By the time Sojourner Truth would have been about 11 years old (1808), the importation of African slaves had become illegal. American slave owners had developed a new industry—breeding slaves and breaking up Black families in order to satisfy the needs of cotton-producing states such as Alabama, where her son was sent.

While the slave trade was quickly becoming illegal in New York, that did not stop pirates such as those affiliated with Dumont from illegally selling slaves to southern plantations by dismantling Black families. Apparently they felt certain that the slaves would not be intelligent enough to challenge them in court. Sojourner Truth herself was sold at least four times from 1810 to 1826.[20] However, Sojourner Truth surprised them. Barefoot and penniless, she sought help from white Quaker friends, who put her in touch with lawyers, who helped her to win her case in the local court. Somewhere in the midst of her struggle, she prayed:

"Oh God, you know how much I am distressed, for I have told you again and again. Now, God, help me to get my son. if you were in trouble, as I am, and I could help you, as you can help me, think I wouldn't do it? Yes, God, you know I would do it. Oh God, you know I have no money, but you can make the people do for me, and you must make the people hear me—don't let them turn me off, without hearing and helping me."[21]

This was a woman who had a special relationship with God. How far did her prayers take her? In the months following her prayer, Dumont and his cohorts were forced by the local court to return the boy to New York to his mother. Even though the boy was emotionally disturbed by then as a result of beatings from the insane slave master to whom he had been sent, his mother was able to nurture him and locate a job for him in New York. Sojourner Truth traveled throughout the country spreading the Gospel and speaking out against slavery. She became one of the chief abolitionists of the 19th century.

Thomas Dorsey. Another historic figure who had a special relationship with God was Thomas Dorsey, known as the father of gospel music. It was 1932. The place was Pilgrim Baptist Church in Chicago. In Dorsey's words:

"I entered the Pilgrim Baptist Church and looked down that long aisle which led to the altar where my wife and baby lay in the same casket . . . My legs got weak, my knees would not work right, my eyes became blind with a flood of tears. There Nettie lay cold, unmoving, unspeaking."[22]

Throughout her pregnancy, his wife had good medical care. Her sister was a nurse. They had lived with Thomas' uncle, a pharmacist. Dorsey had left Nettie just days before, while she was sleeping. Not wanting to awaken her, he had eased into their bedroom to locate his music. He did not realize at the time that he would never see her alive again.

Nettie began labor cramps while Thomas was out of town. However, even though she had a pre-paid arrangement with a hospital for her delivery there, the hospital had no bed available for her. Rather than deliver the baby at another hospital, she asked if she could deliver it at home with a nurse and doctor attending. They telegrammed Thomas Dorsey. When he called home, all he heard were screams, "Nettie is dead! Nettie is dead! Hurry home."[23]

Numbed, a friend drove him back to Chicago where Dorsey arrived before the undertaker removed the body. The family did not allow him to see the body, but he saw his healthy, nine-pound baby. He was shocked to the point of needing a sedative which put him to sleep. The next morning, he heard that his healthy nine-pound son had died during the night, even though the baby was pronounced completely healthy just hours before.

Pain was not new to Thomas Dorsey. He had already experienced the pain of moving from Villa Rica to Atlanta, Georgia as a young boy and being rejected by light complexioned Black people of Atlanta, because of his African features. He had experienced the pain of moving to Chicago and having his music rejected because it was "old time" blues and not the newest "jazz." He had experienced the pain of having his "gospel blues" rejected by mainline Black churches who, at the time, were only interested in singing and hearing white hymns and Europeanized "negro spirituals."[24] However, his career had taken a gradual upturn, and churches were even splitting over the issue of gospel music. Gospel choirs were being organized in churches throughout Chicago and throughout the country, while recordings by Thomas Dorsey were selling all over the world. However, just as his music career was beginning to peak, he encountered the most tragic incident of his life.

There was no explanation for it. It did not make any sense. However, somewhere in the midst of it, Thomas Dorsey prayed:

"Precious Lord, take my hand. Lead me on. Let me stand. I am tired. I am weak. I am worn. Through the storm, through the night, lead me on to the light. Take my hand, precious Lord. Lead me home."[25]

This was a man who fell in love with God. Following this tragedy, he made a dramatic shift from performing and recording both blues and gospel to devoting all of his time to what became known as "gospel" (gospel blues). Dorsey's songs such as "Precious Lord" are now sung in Black churches throughout the world.

The prayers of Richard Allen, Sojourner Truth and Thomas Dorsey are featured in a collection of prayers compiled by Dr. Melvin Washington, *Conversations with God: Two Centuries of Prayers of African Americans*. Washington writes that contact with God, through prayer, has helped African Americans through the experiences of being chattel slaves, through the rise and fall of Reconstruction, through the assault of lynchings gone unpunished, through the Civil Rights Movement and through the backlash against the gains made during the Civil Rights Movement. In Washington's view, prayers such as those quoted here represent the spiritual nature of a despised person who contacted the Divine. Such prayers of Black people are profiles of spiritual intimacy, and they reflect the spirituality involved in emotional healing. Prayer helps to make sense out of what, on the surface, seems absurd.

Falling in Love with God. How can people facing situations such as those described here manage to fall in love with God in the midst of them? Dr. J. Alfred Smith, Sr., in *Falling in Love with God: Reflections on Prayer,* address this question, by presenting guidelines for establishing intimacy with God, regardless of the circumstances of one's life. In this book, Dr. J. Alfred Smith, Sr. indicates that intimacy with God is possible for people of all walks of life—not just for "giants" such as Richard Allen, Sojourner Truth and Thomas Dorsey.

Dr. J. Alfred Smith's book, *Falling in Love with God,* is timely in that, during the coming months, actions taken at both national and state levels of government may catapult thousands of Black people into poverty, homelessness, emotional disturbance and disease. African Americans will be pouring into Black churches in record numbers, trying to make sense out of nonsense, trying to make contact with the Divine, in the midst of life-threatening circumstances. There will be a need for much prayer, and the Black church will become the center where the ministry of prayer will remain critical. Even when people don't have anything, people can cry out to Jesus who has everything. If God could do it for Richard Allen, Sojourner Truth and Thomas Dorsey, God can do it for anyone. Churches throughout the country will want to have prayer ministries which provide sacred spaces for people to reach out and touch the Divine. It is through prayer that this happens.

Structure of the Book, *Falling in Love with God.* In this book, Dr. J. Alfred Smith, Sr. discuss many facets of prayer, in 12 chapters. Preceding each chapter is a short essay, "From the Pastor's Pen" which provides "food for thought" concerning prayer. Following each sermon is a Bible Study Application, developed by Dr. Colleen Birchett, designed to provide a more in-depth study of points made in each chapter.

The book is accompanied by a Leader's Guide which contains discussion guides for each of the 12 chapters of the book. The Leader's Guide also contains answers to the questions posed at the end of each chapter of *Falling in Love with God*. Accompanying the book and the Leader's Guide will be a companion model of a church-wide prayer ministry, which has been installed at Allen Temple Baptist Church, the church of which Dr. J. Alfred Smith is pastor. The model can be adapted and implemented while the book *Falling in Love with God* is being used in group Bible study.

Uses of the Book. The book can be used in group Bible study in local churches, or it can be used for church-wide retreats on prayer. It can be used as a Sunday School elective, and it can be used as a Bible Study Guide for weekday prayer meetings.

The book can also be used in private Bible study, or for family Bible study. One chapter can be studied per month, with one exercise being studied each week. Or one chapter can be studied each week, with individual family members doing separate exercises from a given chapter and reporting their discoveries to the entire group, as homework.

Of course, the overall purpose of the book is to encourage Christians and non-Christians alike to fall in love with God, through a disciplined, consistent and enriching prayer life. Jesus is more than enough!

From the Pastor's Pen

Prayer is like the morning bath that refreshes us after an evening of sleep. Prayer is like the evening bath that cleanses us of the sweat and dirt of working for survival in a compassionless and competitive world. True prayer brings us as we are, with all of our faults and frailties, into the Holy presence of a loving parent who sends us away forgiven, cleaned, renewed, and inspired to live our lives in a world that will soon make us dirty and in need of a new cleansing. You and I pray not because we can; we pray because we must!

Without a bath, we become offensive to others, and above all we cannot live with our own unpleasant odor. Without prayer that cleanses, we are not fit to live with others or ourselves. When we pray, our time of living with God makes our lives with others positive, and our own company with ourselves is the enjoyment of our own privacy.

Leaders who pray will discover that their authority comes not from the visibility of their positions in the public, but their attractiveness and acceptance by the public comes from the fragrance of private time spent alone in the presence of God. May the leader lead others into the delightful discipline of prayer.

Sometimes people lose their passion for prayer when they reach leadership status. They relax and are casual in the prayer, Bible study, and evangelism activities of the church, but they come to planning meetings, business meetings, and those gatherings where secular skills and expertise are needed.

How good it is when we can put aside titles, job descriptions, by-laws, and human-made plans to humble ourselves before God as creatures who need the powerful undergirding and guidance of the Creator.

CHAPTER ONE

PERSONAL SPIRITUAL DEVELOPMENT

"O LORD, thou hast searched me, and known me.
Thou knowest my downsitting and mine uprising, thou understandest
my thought afar off.
Thou compassest my path and my lying down, and art acquainted
with all my ways.
For there is not a word in my tongue, but, lo, O LORD, thou knowest
it altogether.
Thou hast beset me behind and before, and laid thine hand upon me.
Such knowledge is too wonderful for me;
it is high, I cannot attain unto it"

(Psalm 139:1-6, KJV).

INTRODUCTION

You can be an excellent church member without God. You can attend church services, pay your tithes regularly, enjoy church music, and hear sermons without God. You can serve as a leader in the church and you can be popular and well known in the eyes of the local church without allowing the power of God to shape you into a God-like person. You can memorize the words of the Bible until you can quote them to perfection without loving your enemies, and without forgiving those who despitefully use you. You can be a self-righteous person who loves religion without allowing God's love to mature you to spiritual growth that transcends deceit, deception, and divisiveness.

Christian membership and Christian discipleship are two different realities. A church member seeks to satisfy his or her personal agenda through involvement in church activities. A Christian disciple is one who seeks to better understand God's will and who is seeking to prayerfully walk daily with God in a life of evangelism, Christian growth, stewardship, and missionary obedience.

A church member is often negative, critical, and judgmental of others while blindly ignoring his or her own imperfections. A Christian disciple is a happy follower, who in spite of imperfection and injustice, rejoices in the love, mercy, and goodness of God. A church member can be a loose cannon of verbal destruction, whose only testimony is his or her personal hurt; whereas, a Christian disciple testifies to others how God has healed personal wounds, lifted personal burdens of unforgiveness, and has made one stronger than ever before at the broken places. A Christian disciple is God-focused, God-energized, and God-empowered.

A Christian disciple is prayerful; a church member is self-centered. A Christian disciple is Christ-centered; a church member is ego-centered. A Christian disciple is dying daily to self so that Christ might be pre-eminent; a church member wants attention and recognition. A Christian disciple says with John the Baptist, "I must decrease and Jesus Christ must increase."[1] A church member says, "Give me an important seat where I forget my identity, manifest power, and have my unmet status needs satisfied." The Christian disciple says: "Allow me to nourish my soul, to grow spiritually, and to give God the glory. I'd rather be a doorkeeper in the house of my God than to dwell in the tents of the secular world."[2]

In the 19th century, John Ruskin (1819-1900) wrote: "To love is nothing, unless to love is to be known by Him with whom we live."[3] Secular British historian, Arnold J. Toynbee in 1954 wrote: "God is the source from which man derives his significance as well as his consciousness and his life, and the purpose of God that is the reason for man's existence is that the creature should re-enter into communion with its Creator."[4]

The church member ignores God and becomes involved in church activities and in the business of seeking a place under the sun in the eyes of religious society. But God is really the only one who counts. God is the one who supremely matters.

GOD SUPREMELY MATTERS

Not position, not place, not popularity, not power, not politics, but God alone matters, for only God can validate you and me. It is God who gives meaning to human existence and invests it with purpose and dignity. The writer of our text calls you and me to bring ourselves away from self-justification to stand nakedly in the presence of God Almighty. Let us dive into the deep waters of our text as spiritual deep sea divers to discover the treasures that are there for our taking.

The writer of Psalm 139 invites you and me to have an individual encounter with God. You and I are to forget friend, family, and foe. You and I are to ignore prophet, priest, temple, and choir. Each is called to stand alone before God. No excuses can be made. No finger can be pointed at pastor, deacon, trustee, usher, or choir. Without cosmetics or clothes, each is called to meet God individually in the state of spiritual nudity. All scars and unsightly places expose us before the searching eyes of God in our individual Gardens of Eden. God sees you. God sees me. But you and I do not see each other, but God and God alone.

You and I must see God as omniscient or all-knowing. Psalm 139:1-2 presents the truth of God's omniscience: "LORD, you have examined me and you know me. You know everything I do; from far away you understand all my thoughts" (TEV). The Good News translation of verse three tells you and me that God sees every movement. "You see me, whether I am working or resting; you know all my actions." Verse four says that God knows every motive. "Even before I speak, you already know what I will say." Verse six tells you and me that each of us can fool our individual selves, but we cannot fool God.[5]

God knows every movement and motive. God knows every maneuver. You and I try to fool each other with maneuvers on the chessboard or checkerboard of life. But God is a better chess- and checkerboard player. God is a better card player. He knows what cards you and I have in our hand. Look at verse six: "Your knowledge of me is too deep; it is beyond my understanding" (TEV).

In verses 7-10, you and I face head on the truth of God's omnipresence.

"Where could I go to escape from you? Where could I get away from your presence? If I went up to heaven, you would be there; . . . If I flew away beyond the east or lived in the farthest place in the west, you would be there to lead me . . . ." (TEV)

Distance does not hide us from the omnipresent God. Death does not hide us from God's omnipresence. Darkness can't hide us from God. Verse 12b says of Him: "Darkness and light are the same" (TEV).

Verses 13-16 (TEV) remind us of the truth of God's omnipotence. God is all-powerful.

"You created every part of me; you put me together in my mother's womb. I praise you because you are to be feared; all you do is strange and wonderful. I know it with all my heart. When my bones were being formed, carefully put together in my mother's womb, when I was growing there, in secret, you knew that I was there—you saw me before I was born. The days allotted to me had all been recorded in your book, before any of them ever began."

God is standing before you and me. God stands in omniscience, omnipresence, and omnipotence. You and I stand as limited and helpless creatures in need of spiritual transformation. Our minds cannot outwit God. Our legs cannot outrun God. Our arms are too short to box with God.

Here we are uncommitted!

Here we are unloving!

Here we are disobedient!

Here we are finger pointing!

Here we are negative!

What must we do with our two faces of evil? On the one side, there is the face of recklessness, and on the other side, there is the face of cowardice. But God would want us to possess self-control. On the one side, there is arrogance, and on the other side, there is lack of self-confidence. But God would want us to have complete trust in His power to deliver. On the one side, there is vacillation or instability, and on the other side, there is rigidity. But God would want you and me to be open to the leading of the Holy Spirit. On the one side there is wastefulness, and on the other side, there is stinginess. But God would want you and me to be good stewards of tithes and offerings. On the one side, there is laziness, and on the other side, there is busy, busy church work. But God would want us involved in prayer and Bible study. On the one side, there is hypocrisy, but God would want you and me to have compassion. Evil is split into a left-sided and right-sided sinfulness; whereas, God would want you and me to walk on the straight line down the middle of the road. But what is the good news for our predicament?

CONCLUSION

The good news is a prayer for personal, spiritual development. This good news is a treasure in the deep waters of our text. Let us plunge beneath the surface to come up with a new treasure from the ancient biblical Word. Here is the treasure: Pray like you mean it.

"Examine me, O God, and know my mind; test me, and discover my thoughts. Find out if there is any evil in me, and guide me in the everlasting way" (verses 23-24, TEV).

BIBLE STUDY APPLICATION

INSTRUCTIONS: The following exercises can provide a more in-depth understanding of points raised by Dr. J. Alfred Smith, Sr. in this chapter. The biblical references are based on the *King James Version* of the Bible and the Good News Bible.

1. Psalm 139

Psalm 139 is one of many songs people of Israel sang during their worship services.

a. Describe the temple personnel responsible for the music that accompanied the singing of Psalm 139. (1 Chronicles 23:1-5; 25:1-7, 27-31)

b. Describe the musical instruments which accompanied psalms such as Psalm 139. (1 Chronicles 25:1, 3, 6-7; Psalm 33:1-3; 43:4)

c. Describe how the worshipers became involved in the singing of psalms such as Psalm 139. (1 Chronicles 16:36; Psalm 71:22-24)

d. Psalm 139 is divided into four parts. What are the topics of part 1 (verses 1-6) and part 2 (verses 7-12)?

e. What are the topics of Psalm 139, part 3 (verses 13-18) and part 4 (verses 19-24)?

Summary Question: Considering your answers to a-e above, compare and contrast worship services in ancient Israel to those of African American churches today.

2. God's Omniscience and Our Nakedness

Dr. Smith mentions our spiritual nakedness before God and Psalm 139:1-6 mentions that God is omniscient (all-knowing).

a. List at least seven ways in which God knows us. (Psalm 139:1-6)

b. List some ways that Job understood God to be omniscient. (Job 1:1-22; 23:10; 28:20-28)

c. What is another evidence of our nakedness before God? (Psalm 1:6;

37:18-24)

d. What is another evidence of our nakedness before God? (Psalm 94:8-11; Luke 16:15; John 10:14-16)

e. What are some of the other aspects of God's omniscience? (Luke 12:27-31; Romans 8:26-27; 2 Timothy 2:19; 2 Peter 2:9)

Summary Question: Reflect, for a moment, on God's omniscience. Visualize yourself physically, emotionally, and spiritually naked before God. Imagine yourself coming to God like that in prayer. What difference would it make in your prayer life?

3. God's Omnipresence

Verses 7-12 of Psalm 139 emphasize God's omnipresence.

a. List at least six places where God is present. (Psalm 139:7-12)

b. When it comes to God, what does the phrase, "You can run but you can not hide" mean? (Jeremiah 23:23-24; Amos 9:1-6)

c. List at least 10 places where Psalm 104:1-10 says that God is.

d. Name at least five creatures that receive life from the Lord, on a daily basis. (Psalm 104:11-30) What does this suggest about the omnipresence of God?

e. What is a fitting response to the fact of God's omnipresence? (Psalm 104:31-35)

Summary Question: Reflect on God's omnipresence. Visualize yourself doing your weekly activities. Imagine God present with you, giving you and all living creatures life and sustenance. What does this suggest about when and where you can contact God?

4. God's Presence in the Womb

Dr. Smith mentions God as the Creator who knows us because He formed us in our mothers' wombs.

a. What is one record of God's knowledge with the unborn? (Deuteronomy 7:13)

b. What is another record of God's knowledge of the unborn? (Judges 13:2-7,15-24)

c. What is a record of God's interaction with the unborn? (Psalm 22:9-10; Isaiah 49:1, 14-16)

d. Casting Psalm 58:1-5 into 20th century realities, what are some things that can create a rebellious climate within the womb? (See also Isaiah

48:1, 8-11.) Who is partially responsible? What remedy is now available for adversely affected infants? (John 3:16)

e. What is another evidence of interaction between God and the unborn? (Isaiah 46:3)

Summary Question: Reflect on your answers to a-e above. Visualize yourself in your mother's womb and picture God knitting your parts together while interacting with you. How can these images help to produce more intimacy between you and God in prayer?

5. Enemies of God

In Psalm 139:19-22, the enemies of God suddenly appear, changing the focus from intimacy between humans and God.

a. What is one of the chief functions of enemies of God? (Psalm 5)

b. What is another goal of the enemies of God? (Psalm 59:1-2)

c. What is another tactic of the wicked? (Psalm 139:20; Deuteronomy 5:11)

d. What are some other characteristics of enemies of God? (Psalm 31:6; 119:113; 26:4)

e. After the death, burial and resurrection of Christ, what hope is there for the wicked? (Matthew 5:43; John 3:16)

Summary Question: What is the main plea of the psalmist in Psalm 139:23-24? In what sense is the psalmist a role model for us in our prayer lives?

6. Ministry Application

In the first exercise of this Bible Study Application, we explored an image of God's congregation coming before Him with songs and instruments, singing about the omnipotence, omnipresence and omniscience of God. Consider, for a moment, the service which you perform or can perform in your church. To what organization or group do you belong? Visualize that organization coming before God, as a group, in a worship service. Visualize God who sees all, who created each person in his/her mother's womb, and who has all power. What can God do for your group? If God so leads, organize a retreat for the purpose of worshiping God.

7. Personal Application

In what specific ways can the contents of this chapter improve your personal prayer life?

From the Pastor's Pen

At our Thursday, February 19, 1993, Prayer and Bible Study Meeting, large sheets of rain hit the ground with full force, turning their collective liquid into a torrential flood. Nevertheless, the drummer, guitarist, pianist, and a total of 162 persons braved stormy weather for an inspiring prayer service. Prayer coordinators Deacon Jerome Hunt and Deaconess Carolyn Hunt led the group into praying collectively and praying in small groups of three persons.

I was stirred in my thoughts and emotions by the prayers of Deacon Floyd Price. He told God about our fears over the grave economic crisis of the nation. He told God about our large layoffs in California. He asked God to help us with this crisis. He prayed fervently for wisdom and courage to solve the problems facing members whose children have AIDS, and for family unity, and for the improvement of our individual lives. He was passionately and rationally engaged in a priestly and intercessory prayer for you and me. His prayer that reached the ear of God touched the inside of my tender feeling.

All of us traveled home in the rain on freeways fraught with danger, but we were fortified for facing these uncertain days of challenge with inspiration and courage.

Prayer should never be dull and boring. Prayer that is dull and boring is a ritual and routine motivated by oughtness and obligation more than the sheer joy of talking to God whom we love with all our heart, mind, soul, and strength. A real infidelity in our love affair with God is when we do not have time enough to really enjoy God's presence, so that prayer time with God is always too short. True prayer is more than words uttered. True prayer is exciting time spent in God's presence. Can you sense God's presence as you worship or as you sit alone in the stillness of pensive meditation?

When the pain of an illness is too sharp for you to say, "Lord have mercy," or your mind is too downcast and depressed to ask for relief, and when your mind is too confused to reason your way out of the lostness of darkness, God, who hears unuttered thoughts, and who pities every groan, will bring speedy relief with the comfort of a powerful presence. If your adversaries thought you knew the power of prayer, they would say as did Mary, Queen of Scotland: "I fear the prayers of John Knox, more than an army of ten thousand men."

CHAPTER TWO

DISCOVERY
OF LIFE

"Preserve me, O God: for in thee do I put my trust"
(Psalm 16:1, KJV).

INTRODUCTION

N o text in the entire Bible is suited like this one for celebrating the homegoing of Mrs. Gail Marshburn. She was a beautiful woman, blessed with poise, a positive view of life, and a presence that radiated the richness of living consciously in the presence of God. For her, life was to be lived fully in God's eternal now. She knew the meaning of eternal life in both its present and future dimensions.

No one had to explain to Gail Marshburn the meaning of our Lord's words: "I am come that you might have life and have it more abundantly" (John 10:10b, paraphrased).

THE MISDISCOVERY OF LIFE

The late Bertrand Russell was an agnostic philosopher in Great Britain. He used to say: "People are bewildered and don't know how to live a credible life in an incredible world."[1] He spoke of himself and others who never discovered the meaning of life. All around us are people not knowing if life is credible and unable to live a credible life in an incredible world.

Another agnostic was the Viennese philosopher Arthur Schopenhauer. He was a gloomy and depressed person who brooded over his existence. He was unfulfilled, and his life was empty and meaningless. When asked by a police officer, "Who are you and what are you doing here?" he answered, "I wish I knew."[2]

Many persons don't know why God placed them on earth. Some of them call life a nightmare between two nothings and a predicament that precedes death. They agree with atheistic poet Christopher Morley who said, "Life is a foreign language which all men mispronounce.[3] A scientist once said, "Life is a cosmic accident that will someday degenerate back into the void from which it came."[4]

Others experiment with themselves, seeking life through alcohol and drug abuse and the misuse of their bodies through sexual promiscuity and exploitation. Still others fail to find life through excessive spending, self-indulgent accumulation of possessions, risky recreation, or rushing through their days and nights like those in pursuit of that which they are unable to define. They are always looking for life, and they retire each evening without ever finding it.

THE DISCOVERY OF LIFE

Life is found when persons discover the path of life, the joy of God's presence, and those eternal pleasures at the right hand of God. The path of life is Jesus Christ. Jesus taught us about Himself. Of Himself Jesus said, "I am the way, the truth, and the life" (John 14:6, KJV). Gail Marshburn was well acquainted with Jesus Christ. She encouraged me to preach well. She listened with eagerness to hear what I would say about Jesus Christ. Her eagerness to hear the Gospel and to hear me pray made me try very hard to preach well-prepared sermons. Her enjoyment of my public prayers motivated me to pray prayers which were carefully thought out and in harmony with the Scriptures. Her relationship with Jesus was enough to provide her with fullness of joy and pleasures forevermore. Her prayer was:

> *"You have made known to me the path of life;*
> *you will fill me with joy in your presence,*
> *with eternal pleasures at your right hand"*
> (Psalm 16:11, NIV).

An unknown poet tried without success to find the joys and pleasures of life apart from God in Christ. He wrote:

I've tried the broken cisterns, Lord,
but, oh, the fountains failed;
and even as I stooped to drink,
they mocked me as I wailed.
The frail vessels Thou hast made
no hands but Thine can fill;

for the waters of this earth have failed,
and I am thirsty still.

THE CHALLENGE FOR US

We need not make the mistakes of the past. We need not try to drink from broken cisterns. Our challenge is to model our lives after persons like Gail Marshburn whose prayerful discovery enabled them to find new life in Jesus Christ. In this world everything is temporary but Jesus Christ. Jesus Christ is the same yesterday, today, and forever.

I would remind Doctor Janet Marshburn of a resource greater than human-made resources. All human-made resources will fail you. But there is one resource that your mother utilized which never failed you. That resource will sustain you when you miss your mother calling you "pumpkin." That resource is prayer. When you need healing, when you need comfort, when you need counsel, when you need companionship, when you need strength, turn in prayer to God as did your praying mother. At my very first visit, she sat up in the bed and ordered everyone to join hands with her and me, and she peacefully requested that I pray for her and for all in the circle of prayer. She then advised me to take good care of myself. She reminded me to keep on praying.

Because she discovered the path of life, Gail Marshburn, who is now in closer companionship with God, still desires of us to walk with God on earth, prayerfully saying to our Creator, Sustainer, and Redeemer:

"You have made known to me the path of life;
you will fill me with joy in your presence,
with eternal pleasures at your right hand"
(Psalm 16:11, NIV).

CONCLUSION

Two ships were sailing in a harbor, one setting out on a voyage, the other coming home to port. Everyone cheered the ship going out, but the ship sailing in was scarcely noticed. And a wise man said, "Do not rejoice over the ship that is setting out to sea, for you cannot know what storms it will encounter, what fearful dangers it may have to endure. But rejoice over the ship that has safely reached port and brought home all of its passengers in peace."

And this is the way of the world. When a child is born, all rejoice; when a man or woman dies, all weep. We should do the opposite. No one can tell what trials and travails await a child; but when a mortal dies in peace, we should rejoice, for he has completed his long journey, and is leaving this world with the imperishable crown of a good name.

Adapted from the Talmud
A Eulogy of Mrs. Gail Marshburn

BIBLE STUDY APPLICATION

INSTRUCTIONS: The following exercises provide the opportunity to examine more closely, points Dr. Smith makes in this chapter. The Scripture references are based on the *King James Version* and the *Good News Bible*.

1. A Discovery of Joy in Spite of Pain
Dr. J. Alfred Smith mentioned that prayer enabled Gail Marshburn to discover joy in spite of pain. In that sense she had much in common with David, to whom Psalm 16 is attributed.
a. To whom did David look for safety and protection? (Psalm 16:1)
b. From what did David seek protection? (16:2-4; 12:5-8)
c. Among whom did David find pleasure? (16:3; 85:7-9; Hebrews 10:19-25)
d. What was David's portion? (Psalm 16:5; 73:26; 119:55-58; 142:3-5)
e. Where did David find direction for his life? (16:7-11; 62:1-8)

Summary Question: Considering your answers to a-e above, in what ways was Mrs. Marshburn similar to David? What do the lives of David and Mrs. Marshburn teach you about prayer? What evidence is there that they discovered joy in spite of pain?

2. Joy in Sorrow
Psalm 9 is also attributed to David. Notice the title. Evidently this psalm was composed at a very sad moment in David's life.
a. What might the sad occasion of the composition of Psalm 9 have been? (2 Samuel 12:15-20)
b. What caused David's son to die? (2 Samuel 12:13-14)
c. What is the sin to which the Prophet Nathan referred? (2 Samuel 11:1-27)
d. Based on your insights from your answers to a-d above, who was the

oppressed referenced by David? (Psalm 9:9) Who were the wicked? (Psalm 9:17-18)

e. What evidence is there that David found joy in the midst of sorrow? (Psalm 9)

Summary Question: Considering your answers to a-e above, what can you learn from David about discovering joy in the midst of sorrow?

3. Trust in God

Dr. Smith mentioned that Bertrand Russell once said that some people are unable to discover a credible life because life, to them, seems incredible. The prayer of Psalm 59 is evidence that David did not have that problem. Notice the title of this psalm.

a. Without trust in God, what aspects of life might have become overwhelmingly incredible to David? (1 Samuel 18:5-11; 20:1)

b. What aspects of David's life would not "make sense" to most people? (1 Samuel 18:5-11; 20:1)

c. What is one way that David attempted to "make sense" of "nonsense?" (1 Samuel 19:18)

d. What is another more effective way that David made sense out of what was happening to him? (Psalm 59:1-7)

e. What evidence is there that David trusted God? (59:14-16) How did David discover joy in the midst of danger? (59:17)

Summary Question: Considering your answers to a-e above, how did David discover a credible life in spite of the incredible events that surrounded it? What can you learn from David's life?

4. God, Our Refuge

Dr. Smith mentions that through prayer, Mrs. Marshburn and the deacon at his church took refuge in God. Psalm 57 is a prayer attributed to David and set to music. It is evidence that, in times of danger, David took refuge in God. Notice the title of Psalm 57.

a. What danger might David have been facing? (1 Samuel 23:7-8)

b. Where did David go for help? (23:9-12)

c. How does 1 Samuel 23:13—24:3 connect to Psalm 57? (Notice the psalm's title.)

d. How did David's relationship with God influence how he behaved toward

Saul? (Psalm 23; 57)
e. What was the outcome of David's seemingly incredible situation?
(1 Samuel 24:1-22)

Summary Question: Considering your answers to a-e above, what can you learn from David's prayer in Psalm 57? What can you learn from the prayer of the deacon who prayed through a storm? What can you learn about prayer from Mrs. Marshburn who prayed through a terminal illness?

5. Hope

Dr. Smith mentions that Mrs. Marshburn was filled with hope. She and David the psalmist were like ships completing a long journey that had been fraught with dangers. In Psalm 71, David's prayer expresses his discovery of hope in the midst of dangers he faced near the end of his life.
a. What dangers did David face near the end of his life? (Psalm 71:7, 9-11; 2 Samuel 21:15-22)
b. Where did David go for help? (Psalm 71:1-4, 9-13)
c. What is one memory that inspired hope in David? (71:5-6, 17)
d. What is another memory that inspired hope in David? (23)
e. How did David discover hope in the midst of danger? (17:14-25)

Summary Question: Considering your answers to a-e above, what can we learn from the life of David concerning the role of prayer, praise, and thanksgiving during times when the physical body weakens?

6. Ministry Application

Imagine that you were called upon to develop a course to train deacons in ministering to people who were experiencing physical illnesses. How would you use the contents of this chapter to shape the contents of the course? Make a list of weekly topics and related Scriptures for the course.

7. Personal Application

Are you or have you recently experienced a season of suffering, fraught with dangers and perhaps despair? What can you learn from David, who had similar experiences? Make a list.

From the Pastor's Pen

Dietrich Bonhoeffer was respected as a renowned Christian theologian. A theologian thinks critically, coherently, and comprehensively about the concepts and content of Christian doctrine. A theologian muses and meditates on who God is, what God does, and how God relates to persons. A theologian strives to carefully examine Scripture, tradition, and God's continuing communication with us. A true theologian is a powerful person.

It was theologian Bonhoeffer who prayed:

O God, early in the morning I cry to you.
Help me to pray and to concentrate my thoughts on you.
I cannot do this alone.[1]

This simple and humble prayer of Bonhoeffer came from his heart while he was in a Nazi prison during World War II. This prayer may cause you and me to examine our own hearts, simply to see if we spend time each day thinking about God and asking God to help us not lose our focus, concentration, and emphasis on God, since daily distractions and the evil in the world can so easily influence us to live our lives as if a moral, righteous, and caring God did not exist.

CHAPTER THREE

THE PRAYERS OF THE DESPERATE

"They reel to and fro, and stagger like a drunken man, and are at their wits' end.
"Then they cry unto the LORD in their trouble, and he bringeth them out of their distresses"

(Psalm 107:27-28, KJV).

"They stumbled and staggered like drunks—all their skill was useless. Then in their trouble they called to the LORD, and he saved them from their distress"

(Psalm 107:27-28, TEV).

INTRODUCTION

They went out to the sea on their ships. They were not pirates sailing to plunder the wealth of other ships. They were good people trying to earn their living on the sea of life. But bad things happen to people who are trying to do the right thing.

When they sailed their ships deep into the ocean so that land could not be seen behind them, they were greeted by an angry storm in front of them. What had they done to deserve this unfriendly welcome of nature? Why did mean weather mar their trip? Why does the voyage of life surprise good people with weather that is cruel?

Brutal winds slapped them in the face. Falling rain flooded their eyes, blinding their sight. The sharp scent of cold salt water made them sick to the stomach. The flickering lightning that momentarily turned a grey sky red, flashed fear into their hearts. Their feet were wet with water that soaked the floor of their ships. Disturbed at the explosive sound of thunder that sent shivers up and down their spines, they found themselves at their wits' end.

Naughty waves danced to a rhythm that ascended high in the air, then quickly dropped into the depths. As the sea waters continued their stormy dance, the little ships moved helplessly up and down from one side to the other side, carrying occupants whose heads were dizzy with the intoxication of desperation. Without courage, without joy, without the ability to help themselves, they were at their wits' end.

AT WIT'S END

Have you ever been at wit's end? Those who are at wit's end are in trouble, and they do not know how to get themselves out. The little child who is chased by a big bad dog is at wit's end! The student without tuition money to enroll for the next semester is at wit's end! The sick person who is not being helped by the medicine is at wit's end! The adult whose salary is less than his or her living expenses is at wit's end! The concerned parent whose child refuses to take school seriously is at wit's end. The marriage partner whose mate refuses to cooperate and communicate and the employee whose job crisis prevents an environment of peaceful productivity are at wit's end experiences.

Are you standing at "wit's end corner," Christian, with troubled brow? Are you thinking of what is before you and all you are bearing now? Does all the world seem against you as you battle alone? Remember at "wit's end corner" is just where God's power is shown.[2]

Our text reports, at their wit's end:

> "Then they cried unto the LORD in their trouble, and he bringeth them out of their distresses" (Psalm 107:27-28, KJV).

OUR PRAYERFUL LIFESTYLE

Our prayerful lifestyle is necessary in life's voyage for survival. You and I depend too much upon our wits. We say with Henley: "I am the master of my fate. I am the captain of my soul." What arrogance! What nonsense! You and I are at the mercy of the winds and the waves. We cannot hold back the fog, nor can we turn the sky blue. Nor can we prevent a rock hidden beneath the surface of the waters from punching a hole in our ships. Our prayer posture should humble us to say, "Christ is the master of our fate. Christ is the captain of our souls."

Prayer is the safe time when we stand face to face in the holy presence of God. We are always safe in God's holy presence. Children are always safe in the presence of loving and caring parents. It is when we turn our backs and walk away from God's holy presence and from God's principles and precepts and purposes that we end up with destructive relationships and self-created storms in our voyage through life. Remember that you can never stumble when you are on your knees.

Upon rising from our knees, God expects us to live with God's power and walk with those whom God has rescued and redeemed. Our lives should honor God. God rescued you. When the storms of life were raging, God stood by you. Praise God for God's goodness. Let the redeemed of the Lord say so!

Let the redeemed of the Lord praise God for blessing us when we are at our wit's end. Let the redeemed of the Lord praise God for Christ who pilots us through stormy seas. Let the redeemed of the Lord praise God for never allowing us to stumble while we are on our knees.

When in desperation, I, the redeemed of the Lord, I, at my wit's end, will call upon the Lord. He will hear my cry. He will deliver me from distress.

I cannot do it alone. The waves run fast and high, and the fog closes all around, the light goes out in the sky; but I know that we two shall win in the end, Jesus and I.

Coward and wayward and weak, I change with the changing sky. Today so eager and bright, tomorrow too weak to try; but He never gives in, so we two shall win, Jesus and I.

I could not guide it myself, my boat on life's wild sea; there's one who sits by my side, who pulls and steers with me. And I know that we two shall safe enter the port, Jesus and I.[3]

Walk with God in your strength. Just don't pray to God in your weakness. God deserves human relationship in good times and not just in life's storms. The God who saves us in the rough waters of life deserves our obedience. If the wind and the sea obey God's voice, why can't we obey God's commandments? The God who rescues us in trouble, who pilots us a path through troubled waters, who can bring us through thick fogs of uncertainty to a clear view of the land of our destination, is worthy of our dedicated service. This God who is our captain, our compass, our radar, our everything, is worthy of our praise at all times.

CONCLUSION

Praise God for answered prayer. When you were worn out from hard work, when you were living in gloom and darkness, when you were defeated and humiliated, God renewed you. God redeemed you. Praise God.

BIBLE STUDY APPLICATION

INSTRUCTIONS: The exercises below provide an opportunity to examine and study Psalm 107 more closely, along with the points Dr. Smith makes in this chapter. The Scripture references are based on both the *King James Version* and the *Good News Bible*.

1. Prayer of Thanksgiving

Psalm 107 is a prayer of praise to the Lord for aiding people in Israel who had been "at wit's end." Many Bible scholars believe that it was composed after King Cyrus of Persia (Xerxes) allowed Jews who had been scattered throughout the world to return to Jerusalem.

a. What is one way that Israelites had been scattered? (2 Kings 17:5-14)

b. What is another way that Israelites had been scattered? (2 Kings 24:1-2, 5-6, 8-17; 25:13, 18-22; Jeremiah 52:28-30)

c. How widely scattered were the Israelites by the time of the Persian King Xerxes? (Esther 8:1, 3-10)

d. When and how did many Israelites return to Jerusalem? (Ezra 1:1-5)

e. Considering your answers to a-d above, what is the meaning of Psalm 107:1-21, 27-28?

Summary Question: Considering your answers to a-e above, and Psalm 107, what can we learn about the power of prayer in times of distress?

2. A Good Start Aborted

Before the Babylonian exile, the Assyrian invasion of the Northern Kingdom had left Judah, the Southern Kingdom, standing alone. King Josiah ascended to the throne in 640 B.C.

a. What are some reforms that Josiah made? (2 Chronicles 34:3-32; 2 Kings 23:1-19)

b. What one event most dramatically impacted Josiah's reign? (2 Kings 22:8-20)

c. What are some reforms Josiah made in response to Huldah's interpretation of the scroll? (2 Kings 23:1-3, 21-25)

d. What other reforms did Josiah make in response to finding the lost scroll?
   (2 Chronicles 34:33—35:19)
e. What happened after the death of Josiah? (35:23-24; 36:5-14)

Summary Question: Considering your answers to a-e above, what might have caused the Israelites to "reel to and fro" and stagger as drunken men at their wits' end?

3. "At Wit's End"
Psalm 107:27-28 includes a picture of Israelites in chaos and confusion.
   a. In what sense were Israelites caught between the crossfire of Egypt and
      Babylon? (Jeremiah 46)
   b. What is one way that the Israelites felt the impact of Babylon?
      (2 Kings 24:1-7)
   c. What is another way that the Israelites encountered the force of Babylon?
      (Jeremiah 25:18-17)
   d. What further confusion did Zedekiah cause? (Jeremiah 37:1-3, 11-21;
      38:1-28)
   e. What were the "brutal winds" experienced in Jerusalem? (Jeremiah 39:10)

Summary Question: Considering your answers to a-e above, what further meaning is given to Psalm 107:27?

4. A Prayer of the Desperate
Throughout the description of the period of Israel's demise, the Bible includes prayers and prophecies of Jeremiah, the prophet. He writes a prayer of perplexity in Jeremiah 12:1-6.
   a. What is one message God had given Jeremiah? (Jeremiah 11:1-13)
   b. What might have caused Jeremiah to feel perplexed? (11:14-17)
      Why were Jeremiah's "home boys" (Jeremiah 1:1) trying to kill him?
      (11:21) Why might this have been perplexing?
   c. What was the impending disaster? (11:22-23)
   d. In what way did Jeremiah's prayer express desperation? (12:1-4)
   e. What is the evidence of God's promise of compassion for Israel in spite
      of its impending confusion and disaster? (12:5-17)

Summary Question: Dr. J. Alfred Smith says that when we cry to God in desperation, God hears our cry. How is God's answer to Jeremiah an example of this? What can we learn about prayer from this episode in Jeremiah's life?

5. A Prayer of Confidence

Once the Babylonian exile took place, Jeremiah didn't wait until the battle was over. He praised God beforehand. He didn't wait until the people of Israel returned from captivity, he acted as though God had already answered his prayers.

a. What was taking place at the time that Jeremiah placed his trust in God? (Jeremiah 32:1-5, 19-25)

b. How did Jeremiah express his confidence in the Lord? (32:6-25)

c. What was God's response to Jeremiah? (32:26-44)

d. How did God answer Jeremiah's prayers? (Ezra 1:1-2; 2:23, 68-70)

e. What was the first task that the reassembled people set out to do? (3:1-3)

Summary Question: What do your answers to a-e above teach you about the power of prayer?

6. Ministry Application

It is no secret that the African American community is in a state of crisis as it is approaching the threshold of the 21st century. However, the Great Commission of the Black Church (Matthew 28:16-20) remains the same as always. What can your church learn from the Prophet Jeremiah's experience? What can the Black community learn?

7. Personal Application

How does this chapter's contents apply to crises you may be facing in your life?

From the Pastor's Pen

Let us pray:

*O God, help each disciplined disciple
deliberate:*

*to make rough places plain,
and crooked straight;*

*to help the weak; to envy
not the strong;*

*to make the earth a sweeter
dwelling place.*

*In little ways, or if we
may, in great,*

*and in the world to help
the heavenly song,*

*We pray, Lord Jesus, grant
to us thy grace!*[1]

CHAPTER FOUR

PRAYERFULLY COMMUNICATING THE GOOD NEWS

"The Spirit of the Lord is upon me, because he hath anointed me to preach the gospel to the poor; he hath sent me to heal the brokenhearted, to preach deliverance to the captives, and recovering of sight to the blind, to set at liberty them that are bruised, To preach the acceptable year of the Lord"
(Luke 4:18-19, KJV).

INTRODUCTION

Jesus was a peerless preacher and teacher. Jesus, who stood head and shoulder above all who came before or after Him, was matchless in public ministry because He was matchless in His private ministry of prayer.

Mark's Gospel reminds us in chapter one, verse 35, ". . . Rising up a great while before day, he went out, and departed into a solitary place, and there prayed" (KJV). Jesus was baptized and soaked in the spirit world of prayer. Only because of a strong daily life of prayer could Jesus ever say: "The Spirit of the Lord is upon me." If, in each minister or truth-bearer of God, an angel could pour into the genes at birth the courage of Deborah, the eloquence of Frederick Douglass, the political diplomacy of Esther, the intellectual imagination of George Washington Carver, the visionary compassion of Marian Wright Edelman, the administrative mastery of Moses, and the musicality of composers ancient and modern, the multi-talented gifts of ministers and teachers would not last long without the presence and power of a prayer life nourished by the Spirit of God.

No natural talent, no college nor seminary degrees, no ordination credentials, no political connections nor networking with popular preachers and pastors can ever take the place of the nourishment of the Holy Spirit that comes as a result of passionate prayer. Dr. E. Stanley Jones said, "In prayer you align yourself to the purpose and power of God, and through prayer God is able to do things through you that God couldn't do otherwise . . . ."[2]

Fredrick Ward Kates[3] reminds you and me that in prayer our faith reaches up, and God's grace comes down. Prayer is necessary in order to connect with the Holy Spirit. Jesus connected with the Holy Spirit by speaking often to God in prayer.

PRAYERFUL PREACHING AND TEACHING

You who preach and teach must be persons who pray. In order to communicate about God, you must pray to God. You cannot talk truthfully about a person unless you know that person. Prayer helps you to know God in a personal way. The Bible and your college and seminary textbooks give knowledge about God. Prayer gives you a personal experience with God.

You who preach and teach must believe that through prayer the Spirit of the Lord anointed you to preach good news to the poor. The anointing of God's Spirit gives you permission and power to preach and teach.

You who preach and teach have no message of your own. The Spirit of the Lord has anointed you to proclaim good news. You have no good news of your own. No poet or philosopher has good news to pass on to you. That peerless prince, that priceless prophet, and precious priest who also became the bleeding lamb to save us from our sins, that Jesus who is the pioneer and perfecter of our faith, that precious pearl of great price who is a portrait of God, that Jesus is the Good News that you are to preach about.

Prayerfully, lean not on your own understanding as you communicate good news. Remember that you are a Gospel preacher or teacher. The word "Gospel" means "good news." Prayerfully preach good news. Good news blesses and builds. Bad news curses and condemns. Good news is positive and builds up. Bad news is negative and burns down. Good news heals. Bad news wounds. Good news empowers, and bad news disables. Good news provides hope for hopeless situations, strength for times of weakness, forgiveness for times of failure, and good news promises freedom for the prisoners, recovery of sight for the blind, and release and relief for the oppressed.

Only a good news person can truly communicate good news. An ugly, mean, deceitful, selfish, status grabbing, bad news person cannot joyfully tell about the goodness and mercy of God. The good news preacher is a good news person who communicates from the overflow of God's grace in his or her life. The good news communicator says:

"God prepares a table before me in the presence of my enemies . . .
God anoints my head with oil. My cup overflows . . ."
(Psalm 23:5, paraphrased).

It is good news when my cup overflows. My God is not poor; my cup overflows. My God is not cheap; my cup overflows. My God is not stingy; my cup overflows.

Preach good news prayerfully, and leave the results to God. One person prepares the soil. Another sows the seed. Still another cultivates the plant that evolved from the seed. Still another will reap the harvest and will get public recognition for the harvest. But communicating prayerfully is always a venture in faith. Your eloquence, education, and enthusiasm cannot guarantee you a successful career. Even the devil enjoys success. Don't worry about your career. Be faithful to your calling.

CONCLUSION

When adversity comes, pray!
When misunderstood, pray!
When Satan attacks, pray!
When discouraged, pray!
When temptation weakens you, pray!
When you have doubts and fears, pray!

When I become discouraged in my ministry, I walk prayerfully down memory lane to that day of my ordination; it was a Sunday in January. Then I walk farther back in time to that Sunday evening of July 4, 1948, when I first preached a trial sermon. I remember how the Holy Spirit anointed me. I think about how the Holy Spirit has never forsaken or left me. I take new courage whenever I am discouraged. I remember that I have opened my mouth to the Lord, and I cannot go back. I must go, I will go to see what the end will be.

BIBLE STUDY APPLICATION

INSTRUCTIONS: The exercises below provide the opportunity to examine more closely, the points made in this chapter. The Scripture references are based on both the *King James Version* and the *Good News Bible*.

1. Prayer and the Ministry of Jesus

Dr. Smith says that people who minister must be people who pray.

a. What does the Bible reveal about prayer patterns of Jesus during His earthly ministry? (Mark 1:21-38)
b. What did prayer contribute to Jesus' perspective on His ministry? (Matthew 11:25-30)
c. Where did Jesus fit prayer into His busy schedule? (Mark 6:30-46; Luke 5:12-16)
d. How did prayer affect Jesus' decision making? (Luke 6:12-15)
e. What relationship was Jesus to John the Baptist? (Luke 1:36-45) How did prayer help Jesus with personal tragedies that could have distracted Him from His ministry? (Matthew 14:1-13, 23; 11:1-6)

Summary Question: Considering your answers to a-e above, make a list of at least five points of comparison between Jesus' prayer patterns and yours. How can you improve?

2. Prayer and the Anointing

Dr. Smith says that, through prayer, the Spirit of God anoints people to preach.

a. What happened in response to Jesus' prayer at the beginning of His earthly ministry? (Luke 3:21-22)
b. What events followed an extended time of Jesus' praying and fasting? (Luke 4:1-19)
c. What relationship was there between prayer and Jesus' healing ministry? (Mark 7:31-37; Luke 9:28-45)
d. What did prayer have to do with raising Lazarus from the dead? (John 11:1-6, 17, 35, 38-44)
e. How did prayer help Jesus to train the disciples who would carry out His ministry on earth? (Matthew 24:3-14; Mark 13:3-13; Luke 22:24-38)

Summary Question: In response to your answers in a-e above, explain what an anointing is and how it affected Jesus' ministry. What can you learn from this?

3. Prayer and the Will of God

Dr. Smith mentioned that prayer helps us to align ourselves with the will of God.

a. What was the Feast of Unleavened Bread? (Exodus 23:15; Deuteronomy 16:1-4; Matthew 26:17-20)
b. What was the main sacrifice that took place at the celebration of the

Passover? (Exodus 12:1-14)

c. Who would take the place of sacrificial lamb and why? (Hebrews 9:11-15; 10:1-18)

d. How did Jesus prepare to align Himself with God's will? (Matthew 26:36; Mark 14:32)

e. How did Jesus align His will to the will of the Father? (Matthew 26:39; Mark 14:35-39; Luke 22:39-44)

Summary Question: Considering your answers to a-e above, what can you learn from Jesus about handling stresses related to aligning your will with God's will?

4. Prayer and Betrayal

Being betrayed is one of the most painful of experiences. Prayer helped Jesus to deal with betrayal.

a. How did Jesus prepare His disciples for His death? (John 16:17-33)

b. Who was the betrayer among Jesus' disciples? (18:2-3)

c. How did prayer help Jesus to keep the proper perspective about the task He had to accomplish? (17:1-4)

d. How did prayer help Jesus to keep a perspective on the current and future disciples who would abandon Him in His hour of need, but who were assigned to continue His ministry on earth? (17:6-26)

e. What happened when Jesus completed His prayer at Gethsemane? (18:1-11; Matthew 26:39) How had prayer prepared Jesus to respond to this event? (John 18:11)

Summary Question: Considering your answers to a-e above, how did prayer help Jesus to deal with the betrayal that would lead to His death? What can you learn from this about dealing with betrayal?

5. Prayer and the Crucifixion

Jesus prayed as He made His transition through death.

a. Describe the "Kangaroo Court" to which Jesus was taken. (Matthew 26:57-67; 27:1)

b. Describe the various behaviors of people who had been Jesus' disciples. (26:69-75; 27:1-5)

c. How did the government fail Jesus? (27:11-26)

d. List further insults that Jesus encountered. (27:27-44)

e. Discuss the contents of two prayers that Jesus prayed while He endured the pain of the events of a-d above. (Luke 23:34; Matthew 27:46) In what sense do these prayers represent both the human and divine aspects of Christ?

Summary Question: What can you learn from Jesus about praying, under stress and through terminal illnesses?

6. Ministry Application

Develop a six-week Bible study to train people in a prison ministry that deals with prisoners on death row, most of whom say they are innocent. Make a list of six weekly topics, based on the contents of this chapter.

7. Personal Application

What can you learn from the earthly ministry of Jesus about prayer? How do you plan to use it to improve your prayer life?

From the Pastor's Pen

Living the disciplined Christian life is not easy. One can begin the day feeling very close to God. But the nervous energy of a frustrated person, the careless word of a thoughtless person, or an unexpected happening can ruin what peace and poise one had at the dawn of the day. Such unexpected intrusions into a person's life can distort one's perspective and erode one's spirituality. This prayer from anonymous lips is a help to you and me.

O make me patient Lord,
Patient in daily cares;
Keep me from thoughtless words,
that slip out unawares.
And help me, Lord, I pray,
Still nearer thee to live,
And as I journey on,
More of thy presence give.[1]

CHAPTER FIVE

PRAYERS FOR ANGRY PEOPLE

"Be ye angry, and sin not: let not the sun go down upon your wrath: Neither give place to the devil"
(Ephesians 4:26-27, KJV).

"A fool uttereth all his mind: but a wise man keepeth it in till afterwards. An angry man stirreth up strife, and a furious man aboundeth in transgression"
(Proverbs 29:11, 22, KJV).

INTRODUCTION

It was Thursday, July 1, 1993. The place was 101 California Street, San Francisco, California. Just before 3:00 p.m., a gunman walked into the 34th floor offices of the law firm of Pettit and Martin with three semi-automatic pistols and began shooting. He wounded six persons, and he killed eight persons before killing himself as police closed in on him. Was it anger or was it insanity, or was it both that caused this man to commit mass murder, destroy himself, and hurt innocent families?

Anger and insanity are on the loose in American society. On October 16, 1991, 23 people were fatally shot by George Hennard who drove his pickup truck through a plate glass window at Luby's Cafeteria in Kileen, Texas. On July 18, 1984, 21 people were fatally shot in a McDonald's restaurant in San Yisidro, California by James Oliver Huberty, an out-of-work security guard. On August 20, 1986, four people were shot to death at a post office in Edmond, Oklahoma by Pat Sherrill, a postal worker who was angry because he was about to be fired. On January 17, 1989, Patrick Purdy, an angry and troubled young man, took out his anger and confusion on a school yard in

Stockton, California with an AK-47 semi-automatic weapon. Five children were killed and 29 were wounded. Patrick Purdy then killed himself with a pistol. Innocent families are suffering from the anger and insanity of a young man consumed by the anger and evil that lived in his soul.

THE VISITATION OF ANGER

Anger has moved into the neighborhood of our minds. The gentle word, the gentle feeling, the gentle gesture, the gentle approach, and the gentle spirit have all moved out of the neighborhoods of our mentality and spirituality. Anger, hostility, revenge, and insanity have moved in, depreciating the property values of morality, turning our mental neighborhoods into violent and angry ghettos.

Anger visits each one of us. Anger visits saints and sinners. Anger and aggression visit as human responses to discomfort, tension, pain, frustration, and injustice. The hungry or wet baby in a crib or the senior adult disrespected by a younger generation that does not know God can testify to justifiable feelings of anger. This is why the Scripture text does not put down all anger. Some anger may be justifiable.

The text does call attention to the use which is made of anger. The use of anger can be creative or destructive. This is what the text says:

> "Be ye angry, and sin not: let not the sun go down upon your wrath: Neither give place to the devil" (Ephesians 4:26-27, KJV).

When anger visits you, it seldom comes as a helpful friend. Anger visits you as a false friend who deceives you. How does anger exploit hurt and pain with sly and deceptive suggestions and motivations? First of all, anger is usually self-centered in its focus and causes you to think that you alone are the victim. Anger blinds you to the hurt and pain all around you, and anger blindfolds you so that you cannot see that either by the sin of omission or commission, or by the sin of neglect and neutrality, you, too, share in the collective sin of causing or nourishing injustice.

Anger blinds you from seeing your blessings. Instead of being grateful for what you have and who you are, anger misleads you into being ungrateful for the good things you have in life and for who you are and what you can become. Not only does anger create self-centeredness and ingratitude, it produces bitterness and self-destruction.

Do not let the sun go down while you are still angry. Do not go to sleep at night with anger, and do not spend sleepless nights nourishing your anger. Don't wake up in the morning with anger. You don't want to feed anger the breakfast of evil thoughts. If you continue to nourish anger, it will produce children of bitterness and grandchildren of self-destruction.

This is why Scripture says:

"A fool uttereth all his mind: but a wise man keepeth it in till afterwards" (Proverbs 29:11, KJV).

Anger is not only divisive, it is also diversionary. Anger is divisive because it produces division, dissension, and destruction. Anger destroys long-standing relationships. Anger is diversionary because it takes your focus off your mission and purpose for life. Anger does not allow you to be positive, productive, and progressive. Anger stalls your forward mobility. Anger behaves like gravity and prevents your upward mobility with the downward pull of negativity. Anger is like ice that freezes the potential flow of inspiration toward the attainment of objectives and goals. Anger is both divisive and diversionary.

Anger not only robs you of your personal joy for living and serving, but anger drives others away from you. Angry people are unattractive people. Only the devil and his crowd enjoy fellowshiping with the angry person.

CONCLUSION

Since anger is destructive and counterproductive, let us find the joy that comes from genuine Christian service. Joy also takes the place of anger when we rejoice over the fact that we are no longer enemies of God. We have been forgiven. Since God has forgiven us, let us forgive one another. Let us remember that the joy of the Lord is our strength.

BIBLE STUDY APPLICATION

INSTRUCTIONS: The following exercises provide the opportunity to study more closely, points made by Dr. Smith in this chapter. The Biblical references are based on both the *King James Version* and the *Good News Bible*.

1. Sources of Anger

Dr. Smith mentioned that there are many legitimate reasons for anger. Oppression is often a source of anger.

a. What was one source of oppression for people living in Galilee?

(Matthew 4:23-24)

b. What was another source of oppression for Galilean "sharecroppers?" (Mark10:17-23)

c. What was another possible source of anger among many Galileans? (6:30-44)

d. What are some other possible sources of anger? (Matthew 22:15-17; Luke 5:1-5; John 21:3)

e. What are some biblical strategies for dealing with anger? (Matthew 5:1-2, 21-25; Ephesians 4:26-29)

Summary Question: Considering your answers to a-e above, are there any parallels between life among Galilean and life among African Americans today? What can we learn from these passages of Scripture about handling anger today?

2. Outcomes of Unmanaged Anger

There are a number of angry people who surface in the pages of the Bible, ruining their lives because of anger.

a. What was one outcome of unmanaged anger in the family of Isaac and Rebecca? (Genesis 27:41-46)

b. What was one outcome of Saul's anger? (1 Samuel 18:6-9; 19:1-3, 9-11)

c. What are some outcomes of anger manifested in the life of Samson? (Judges 15:1-8)

d. What was an outcome of anger in the life of King Xerxes? (Esther 1:1—2:4)

e. What does the Bible say about uncontrolled expressions of anger? (Proverbs 15:1, 18; 22:8; 14:17)

Summary Question: Considering your answers to a-e above, how can you apply these insights to your life?

3. Angry Prayers

The Bible contains examples of people who came to God in anger.

a. Why was Moses angry? (Numbers 11:1-15) How did God respond? (11:16-17)

b. Why was David angry? (Psalm 6) What changed his disposition?

c. Why was the author of Lamentations angry? (Lamentations 1:1-3, 20-21; 3:55-66) What calmed the author?

d. Nineveh was the capital of Assyria, a menace to the Israelites. Why was

Jonah angry? (Jonah 4:1-4; 3:10; 2 Chronicles 32:1-10) What was God's response? (Jonah 4:4-11)
e. Why was Habakkuk angry? (Habakkuk 1:1-4, 12—2:1) What was the Lord's response? (1:5-11; 2:2-4)

Summary Question: What do all of these prayers have in common? What do all of God's responses have in common? What can we learn from these situations and from God's responses?

4. Guidelines for Dealing with Anger

Dr. Smith says that anger visits each of us.
a. What is the best thing to do with anger? (Proverbs 16:32) Why?
b. How should one respond to a person with an uncontrolled temper? (22:24) Why?
c. How can one avoid evoking anger in others? (25:23)
d. What is one danger of "hanging out" with quick-tempered people? (29:22)
e. What is a sign of foolishness? (Ecclesiastes 7:9)

Summary Question: How can you apply insights from a-e to your life? What does this have to do with prayer?

5. New Testament Teachings on Anger

Dr. J. Alfred Smith says that anger can blind us from seeing our blessings.
a. What must Christians do with anger? (Ephesians 4:29-32) Why? (Ephesians 4:14-16)
b. For what purpose should Christians put away anger? (Colossians 3:1-8)
c. How does one deal with anger while parenting? (Colossians 3:20; Ephesians 6:4) Why?
d. What is a constructive way of handling anger? (Ephesians 4:26-29)
e. What is another constructive way of handling anger? (Matthew 5:23-24)

Summary Question: How can you apply insights from a-e above to your life?

6. Ministry Application

Prepare an outline of a Bible study class for married couples, based on the content of this chapter. List weekly topics for a 10-week class.

7. Personal Application

What is the most important point presented in this chapter that applies to your life? How do you intend to apply it?

From the Pastor's Pen

What can you and I do to bring the sacred into our secular world? What can you and I do to remind ourselves and those whose lives we touch on a daily basis that the holy and hallowed invisible presence of God confronts our pagan and profane world through the Spirit of Christ that is in us? To what extent does Jesus Christ live in us? By failing to maintain a prayerful mind, are we shutting out of our lives the presence and power of Jesus Christ?

Prayer assures you and me that Christ is always in control of our motivations, mental reflections, and moral behavior as we move about in a world that rejects the morality and mind of Jesus Christ.

The Protestant reformer, Martin Luther, speaks prayerfully as we should speak in his much loved hymn, "Dear Christians, One and All:"

To me he said: Stay close to me.
I am your rock and castle.
Your ransom I myself will be;
For you I strive and wrestle;
For I am yours, and you are mine,
and where I am you may remain;
The foe shall not divide us.[1]

Let no foe tempt us to believe that we are too busy to pray, and by praying let us make visible in ourselves the redemptive and reconciling presence of Christ in our alienated and unreconciled world.

CHAPTER SIX

A PRAYER THAT IS GREATER THAN GREAT

"Thy kingdom come. Thy will be done in earth, as it is in heaven"
(Matthew 6:10, KJV).

INTRODUCTION

Most prayer is mediocre. A few prayers are great. Very few prayers are greater than great. A mediocre prayer is a self-centered prayer in which a human, a beggar, troubles God for a meager handout. The great prayer is a lofty and unselfish request to bless others. Such was Solomon's prayer (1 Kings 3:5-9). Instead of asking for increased wealth and additional power, Solomon prayed for wisdom and knowledge to lead God's people. The prayer that is greater than great comes from the heart of any person who sincerely asks God to take charge of the world and run it, even if all of the people in the world are unhappy with the way that God runs things.

THE KINGDOM OF GOD

The Greek word *basileia* means "reign" or "kingdom" or "the act of reigning" rather than "the place of reigning." The reign of God is a technical phrase for the idea of the rule of God over history.

What if God were in charge of modern history? Imagine how the six o'clock television news would change. Imagine how newspaper headlines would change. If God takes over the managing of your life, what changes would take place? What if we could imagine God running our lives, our families, our businesses, our churches, schools, and governments; and what would take place if you and I stopped imagining and really permitted God to manage our lives and our world? To really pray, "Your kingdom come," and then step back after praying this prayer so that God could really do what you and I asked God to do, is to pray a prayer that is greater than great.

Those who claim Christ as their king must act like Christ is their King. To do otherwise is to make prayer less than great and less than good. Spiritual rulership with Christ as King was never based on the constitutional monarchy of medieval history. Of those times Karl Mannhein said: "The King reigns but does not govern." Jesus Christ does not occupy the throne of the human heart if He is not allowed to reign.

Whenever we attempt to pray the prayer that is greater than great, demonic powers invade our space to sit in the mental and moral places that belong only to Jesus Christ.

THE INTRUSION OF THE DEMONIC

The demonic seeks to replace the angelic with innocent manifestations of evil thoughts. Evil thoughts give birth to evil acts. Evil acts produce evil deeds. Evil deeds mature into evil characters. Evil characters mask evil personalities behind the rhetoric and ritual of religious worship. The intrusion of the demonic can come to us as Satan dressed in garments of light, or the demonic can storm the altar of the human heart with the violence and meanness of poisonous snakes and scorpions. But Jesus promised His disciples victory over the evil in this world.

> *"The seventy-two returned with joy and said, 'Lord, even the demons submit to us in your name.' He replied, 'I saw Satan fall like lightning from heaven. I have given you authority to trample on snakes and scorpions, and to overcome all the power of the enemy; nothing will harm you. However, do not rejoice that the spirits submit to you, but rejoice that your names are written in heaven.'"* (Luke 10:17-18, NIV).

As citizens who trust God faithfully, let us claim the victory over all evil forces that would defeat, destroy, or displace us in God's kingdom. God has granted us authority and power for victorious living. Let us use God's authority and power. God's kingdom of righteousness, justice, and peace on earth is always underpopulated.

KINGDOM RECRUITMENT

Everywhere you travel on earth, the kingdom of evil suffers from overpopulation. You name the places. Visit the municipal and federal courts; visit the juvenile halls and detention centers. Visit the prisons, the halfway houses and recovery and rehabilitation centers. Visit the broken homes and visit the streets where broken lives gather on the corners of the alone, the forlorn, and the lost. Visit the places where addicts become AIDS victims, and innocent youth have their lives tarnished by sin. Visit the temples of pleasures and visit the temples of materialism where people spend money for the body while starving their souls. At these places and still more places you will see the demonic staff of Satan recruiting souls to overpopulate the kingdom of evil.

But you and I are recruiters for Jesus Christ. We have good news to share. We want lost souls saved and sin-sick souls healed. That is why we pray the prayer that is greater than great: "Your kingdom come."

BIBLE STUDY APPLICATION

INSTRUCTIONS: The following exercises provide the opportunity to study more closely, the points raised by Dr. Smith in this chapter. The Biblical references are based on both the *King James Version* and the *Good News Bible*.

1. Solomon

Dr. J. Alfred Smith mentioned the prayer of Solomon as an example of one who wanted God's will to be done on earth.

a. Where did Solomon fall among the sons of King David? (2 Samuel 12:24; 5:13-16; 1 Chronicles 3:1-8; 14:4-7) How was it that a "middle child" was selected as king over his older brothers? (1 Kings 1:32-40)

b. What "charge" was given to Solomon upon ascension to the throne? (1 Kings1:47; 2:1-9)

c. What was one major task that Solomon was to accomplish? (1 Chronicles 22:1-13; 1 Kings 8:14-16)

d. What are two steps that King David took before Solomon ascended to the throne? (2 Samuel 21:1-22)

e. What resources did David leave for Solomon? (2 Samuel 23:8-23; 1 Chronicles 22:14-19; 23—27; 29:1-5)

Summary Question: Some biblical scholars believe that Solomon was younger than 20 years of age when he ascended to the throne of Israel. Based on your answers to a-e above, and in your own words, describe the awesome challenge that a person of that age faced.

2. The Intrusion of the Demonic

Dr. J. Alfred Smith mentions how frequently evil forces attempt to defeat, destroy, and displace the implementation of God's plans and God's kingdom.

a. What form did evil forces take at the beginning of Solomon's reign? (1 Kings 1:1, 4; 2:13-22)

b. Why might Adonijah's request have been inappropriate? (1 Kings 1:1-5; 2:17; 2 Samuel 3:7; 12:8; 16:20-23)

c. Why was it necessary to eliminate Abiathar? (1 Kings 1:19; 2:26-27; 1 Samuel 2:31-35)

d. Why was it necessary to eliminate Joab? (1 Kings 2:5, 28-34; 1:7, 15; 2 Samuel 18:1-17; 2 Samuel 19:8-14; 20:1, 4-13)

e. Why was it necessary to eliminate Shimei? (2 Samuel 16:5-14; 1 Kings 2:8)

Summary Question: Reconsider your answers to b and d above, and to Exercise #1 in this chapter. What was Satan, through Adonijah, attempting to disrupt?

3. A Prayer for Wisdom

In the context of the circumstances revealed in Exercises #1 and #2, Solomon prayed. He reached out to God for wisdom to lead God's people.

a. Where did Solomon go to pray? (1 Kings 3:4) What was the significance of this town? (Joshua 9:3-27; 18:21-25; 21:17)

b. What is another reason that Gibeon was important? (1 Chronicles 16:39; 2 Chronicles 1:2-6)

c. What sin had been committed at Gibeon? (2 Samuel 21:1-9)

d. For what did Solomon ask the Lord? (1 Kings 3:9) Why was wisdom or discernment so important for Solomon? (Deuteronomy 1:9-18; 1 Kings 3:16-28)

e. What are some examples of evidence that God answered Solomon's prayer for wisdom? (1 Kings 3:16-28; 5:1-5)

Summary Question: Dr. J. Alfred Smith mentions the significance of advancing God's will on earth. What influence did Solomon's gift of wisdom have on the fulfillment of God's ultimate plan? (Matthew 1:1-11; Revelation 5:6-14) What can we learn about prayer from Solomon's prayer?

4. A Prayer for Dedication

Solomon saw the construction of the temple as central to the fulfillment of God's plan on earth.

a. In your own words, briefly describe some features of the beauty of the temple Solomon built. (1 Kings 6:1-36)

b. Solomon thanked God for fulfillment of God's plan. In what sense was construction of the temple a fulfillment of God's promise? (1 Chronicles 22:1-13; 1 Kings 8:14-20)

c. What other promise did Solomon want God to fulfill? (1 Kings 8:25-26) What is one sense in which one aspect of God's promise eventually was not fulfilled? (2 Kings 17:5-12) In what ways was the promise kept? (John 1:12; Romans 1:16; 10:12-17; Galatians 3:28; Colossians 3:11; Hebrews 9:23-28; Revelation 5)

d. What significance did Solomon, in his prayer to God, place on prayer? (1 Kings 8:27-30) What concern did he have for justice? (8:31-32)

e. What are some requests of Solomon that were eventually granted by God? (1 Kings 8:33-34; Ezra 1:1-2; 2:1-2; 1 Kings 22:39-41; 2 Kings 19; 2 Chronicles 14:11; 20:20)

Summary Question: Considering your answers to a-e above, what role did Solomon's prayers play in the fulfillment of God's plan and will on earth?

5. The Kingdom of God

Dr. Smith mentions that Christians should be involved with recruiting people into the kingdom of God. The Bible contains many images of the kingdom of God.

a. In one sense, the kingdom of God is anywhere that God and His children are. Explain. (Psalm 90:1-2; 102:24-28; 44:6-8)

b. In another sense, the kingdom of God is a spiritual kingdom whose characteristics will be revealed fully in the future. What is the image of this kingdom of God that was revealed through Isaiah? (Isaiah 65:17-25)

c. What vision of the kingdom of God was revealed through Jeremiah? (Jeremiah 31:31-34)

d. How did Jesus describe the future kingdom of God? (Matthew 8:10-12; 25:31-46)

e. After the death, burial, and resurrection of Christ, how does one become a citizen of the kingdom of God? (John 1:12; James 2:5; Colossians 1:13; Acts 14:22; 16:31; Matthew 25:34)

Summary Question: Dr. J. Alfred Smith says that we should be actively recruiting people into the kingdom of God. What steps can you take to recruit people for the kingdom? What would prayer have to do with it?

6. Ministry Application

Solomon considered it of great importance for the temple of the Lord to be a beautiful place where people could come to make contact with the Divine. List ways in which you church can beautify your church building and ways to inform people that they are welcome.

7. Personal Application

What is the most important thing that you can learn from Solomon about prayer? How do you intend to apply it to your life?

From the Pastor's Pen

Let us become missionaries of courage. Let us pray for gun control. Let us become vocal and politically active in promoting nonviolence and peace. Jesus Christ taught:

"Blessed are the peacemakers:
for they shall be called the children of God" (Matthew 5:9, KJV).

As children of God, you and I cannot be happy about the random, multiple shootings that occur in our city. People of every race and social class have lost family members and friends from assault weapons.

The National Rifle Association says: Guns don't kill; people kill. This is a false statement. The truth is people kill other people with guns! Let us pray for the courage to stand up for gun control. Let us work and pray for safe living.

Jesus taught us to pray not only about individual concerns and needs, but also to pray for the well-being of the collective good of society. Maturity in our prayer life expresses a broad and unselfish interest in the enriching of societal values as promoted and preserved by institutions and governmental agencies and structures. This is why we pray: "Thy kingdom come. Thy will be done in earth, as it is in heaven" (Matthew 6:10, KJV).

Dwight Hopkins, in his book, Shoes That Fit Our Feet,[1] addresses the need for a spirituality that will speak to unraveling demonic and inhibiting systems that strangle the realizing of our spiritual potentiality on a personal and societal level. He quotes Martin Luther King, Jr., who said:

Any religion that professes to be concerned
about the souls of persons, and is not concerned
about the slums that cripple the soul,
the economic conditions that stagnate the soul,
and the city governments that may damn the soul
is a dry, dead, do nothing religion in need of new blood.

CHAPTER SEVEN

PRAYER FOR BETTER TIMES

"Hear me when I call, O God of my righteousness: thou hast enlarged me when I was in distress; have mercy upon me, and hear my prayer" (KJV).

"Answer me when I call to you, O my righteous God. Give me relief from my distress; be merciful to me and hear my prayer" (NIV).

"Answer me when I call, O God of my night! Thou hast given me room when I was in distress. Be gracious to me, and hear my prayer" (RSV).

Psalm 4:1

INTRODUCTION

Better times are needed. Better times are better than bad times, evil times, or worse times. Better times are better than these times.

This prayer of King David is your prayer and my prayer. David, like you and me, was an at-risk person. He was about to be destroyed sometime between January and December by the evils that make the better good, and the good the worst of times. So David appeals not to friends or foes, not to law enforcement or the judicial system of the courts, not to any human structure of relief or intellectual body on problem solving. David, in deep, deep, turmoil turns to God. No doctors, no lawyers, no bankers, no job supervisors, no counselors, psychologists, or prayer partners, nobody but God can answer prayer! Why then do we spend so little time living prayerfully in God's prayer-hearing presence?

OUR TIMES

Our times demand that we spend quality time praying in the prayer-hearing presence of God. During the week of January 3-10, 1993, our hearts rejoiced when, at the first prayer meeting of the year, one college-aged male was baptized, two boys between the ages of seven and 11 became candidates for baptism, and one adult lady united on the basis of her Christian experience. But two families had sons who were murdered, one innocent teenage girl was kidnaped, and death reduced our church's membership through sickness and disease. Our times could be better. These are bittersweet times.

David's prayer can help us as we pray for better times. Let us study David's prayer. Let us make his prayer our prayer. Let us study David's prayer in three translations: The *King James Version*, the *New International Version*, and the *Revised Standard Version*. Each translation has three emphases.

OUR BIBLICAL TEXT

The text is from Psalm 4:1, and it is a prayer that you and I can pray. David's son, Absalom, had turned against him. His own army was now under Absalom's control and was about to help Absalom destroy him. Ahithophel, the priestly prophet of God, was even against David.

THE KING JAMES VERSION EMPHASIS

1. Unanswered mail and unreturned telephone calls. How does it feel to be ignored, to be placed last on the list of priorities, or on a "do nothing about it" list?
2. God's loving care has always filled me when I was troubled.
3. Be kind to me, God. Hearing my prayer is important; I need You.

THE NEW INTERNATIONAL VERSION EMPHASIS

1. Articulates God's urgent response that matches our urgency of request. A plea that God will take us seriously when we pray.
2. A cry for relief from distress allows the stormy weather to subside, permits the pressures to diminish and gives a relief from the hot rays of the burning sun; we need relief from problem after problem.
3. Even if we do not deserve relief, be merciful unto us and grant it, O righteous God. As a righteous God, You do not seek to even the score.

THE REVISED STANDARD VERSION EMPHASIS

1. Present salvation is based on past redemption. God, because You blessed us in times past, bless us again because You are our only salvation.

2. Give us room, O God. Our troubles are crowding in on us. We are cramped and almost crushed by tribulation. We need the space of Your mercy.
3. Be gracious unto us.

CONCLUSION

We may be an ungracious people. We may have refused grace to others who needed grace, mercy to others who needed mercy, and forgiveness to others who needed forgiveness. We may have refused a second chance or a third and fourth chance to others who were at the risk of being destroyed by our revenge. We may have turned a deaf ear to those who fell on their knees to us and pleaded for their lives, their happiness, their peace. But now, Lord, since we are in their shoes, be gracious unto us as was Your Son, who prayed: "Father, forgive them; for they know not what they do" (Luke 23:34, KJV). Justice we deserve. But grace is what we need! O God of our night, hear our prayer!

BIBLE STUDY APPLICATION

INSTRUCTIONS: The following exercises provide the opportunity to study the points raised by Dr. Smith in this chapter more closely. The biblical references are based on both the *King James Version* and the *Good News Bible.*

1. God's Promises: Prayer

Dr. J. Alfred Smith says that David cried out to God for better times. The Bible contains many promises of God concerning outcomes of prayers such as that of David.

a. What can we expect from God if we ask for what we need?
(Matthew 7:7, 8; 21:22; John 15:7)

b. How does God respond to our prayers? (Isaiah 30:19; 65:24; 1 John 5:14, 15; Jeremiah 29:12)

c. What happens when we ask in Jesus' name? (John 16:23, 24)

d. What happens when we cry unto the Lord? (Psalm 55:17; 145:18, 19)

e. What happens when we pray for others? (James 5:16)

Summary Question: Review the major points that Dr. Smith makes in this chapter. How do your answers to a-e relate to what to Dr. Smith says? How do the insights gained from your answers relate to your prayer life? How do they relate to dealing with times of trouble?

2. Prayers in Times of Trouble

Dr. Smith points out that we are living in a time of trouble.

a. What should we do when trouble comes? (Psalm 50:14-15)

b. What perspective should we have on our troubles? (Psalm 42)

c. Why should we go to God when we are in trouble? (46:1-7)

d. Is any request insignificant to God? (Psalm 138)

e. In what sense do we respond differently to troubles than evil people do? (2 Timothy 2:8-13)

Summary Question: Considering your answers to a-e above, what does Dr. Smith mean when he says, "Our times demand that we spend quality time praying in the prayer-hearing presence of God"?

3. Enemies

King David, author of Psalm 4, had many enemies. Yet he prayed in the midst of the trouble they caused for him. The Bible contains many promises of God concerning our reactions to enemies.

a. Why does it not make sense to fear what enemies can do? (Psalm 37:27-29, 40)

b. What does God promise regarding our enemies? (Proverbs 16:7)

c. Can enemies inflict serious harm on a righteous person? (Isaiah 54:15-17; Hebrews 13:5-8) Why not?

d. What dangers do enemies of God's people face? (Job 8:22; Deuteronomy 20:4; 28:7)

e. What does it mean if God does not seem to be coming when we want Him? (Habakkuk 2:1-4; Luke 18:7)

Summary Question: This book is being published during a time when dozens of African American and integrated churches have been bombed. Considering this reality, and your answers to a-e above, what does Dr. Smith mean when he says, "Our times demand that we spend quality time in the prayer-hearing presence of God"?

4. Poverty

Enemies of African Americans and of God's people everywhere are taking actions to plunge millions of people into homelessness and poverty. However, the Bible contains many promises concerning those who are oppressed in this way.

a. Who gives power to improve economic situations? (Deuteronomy 8:18;

Psalm 113:7)
b. Where does the hope of the poor really lie? (Job 5:12-16; Psalm 9: 17-20; 132:15)
c. How does the Lord react to those who are oppressed? (72:12-14; 37:25-26)
d. What should be the disposition of those who are oppressed? (Matthew 6:31-34)
e. What promises are in the Bible concerning how people who have money are to respond to those who do not? (Psalm 41:1, 2; Luke 6:38; 14:13, 14; Proverbs 14:21)

Summary Question: Dr. Smith says that these are bittersweet times. What does he mean? How do the insights in exercises a-e above relate to what Dr. Smith has said?

5. Fear
In recent years there has been an escalation of terrorism. This has caused fear to run rampant in communities throughout America. However, the Bible contains many promises regarding fear.
a. What is the best cure for fear? (Proverbs 1:33; Isaiah 54:14)
b. Why should the Christian not be afraid? (41:13)
c. What is the foundation of our response to terrorism? (Matthew 10:28; Proverbs 3:25, 26)
d. What can be said to soothe the pain of those who have lost their loved ones due to terrorism? (Isaiah 14:3; 1 Peter 3:12-14; Psalm 46:1)
e. What helps us to look beyond those who attempt to bind us in fear? (Proverbs 29:25; Psalm 91:4-6; Isaiah 54:4; 43:2; John 14:27; Revelation 21)

Summary Question: How can the Scripture passages in a-e above help you in dealing with fear?

6. Ministry Application
Design a ministry at your church that involves praying, reflecting and acting in response to specific issues facing the community surrounding it..

7. Personal Application
Select the most important insight you gained from the study of this chapter. How do you plan to apply it to your life?

From the Pastor's Pen

The gravity of evil always seems to be stronger than the upward surge of wind that enables us to fly above the sinful mediocrity of the masses. But as a large airliner carrying tons of weight moves upward against the downward tug of gravity, so can we rise upward carrying all of our heavy burdens with the powerful jet propulsion of the Holy Spirit. Such power results from persistent and consistent praying for empowerment for victorious Christian living.

The time you and I spend uselessly robs us of the time that is required to develop prayer power for the upward climb against the negative gravitational forces that pull us down to defeat, discouragement, and disgrace.

This is why Dr. Jesse Jai McNeal in As Thy Days So Thy Strength, prayed:

O merciful and strong God, give me a spirit
which will transcend every outward limitation of my body.
Make me free within that no time or place or condition of life
may conquer my spirit. With body and spirit consecrated to Thee,
arm me with the strength to obey Thy blessed will;
for Jesus' sake.[1]
Amen.

CHAPTER EIGHT

THE PRAYER TRADITION OF BLACK PEOPLE

"O give thanks unto the Lord; call upon his name: make known his deeds among the people. Sing unto him, sing psalms unto him: talk ye of all his wondrous works. Glory ye in his holy name: let the heart of them rejoice that seek the LORD. Seek the LORD, and his strength: seek his face evermore."
(Psalm 105:1-4, KJV)

INTRODUCTION

Black history reveals a rich prayer tradition. Dr. Harold Carter reminds us of our rich spiritual tradition in his work, *The Prayer Tradition of Black People*. In his work, *The Black Presence in the Bible*, the Reverend Walter McCray tells us, "Black people need to understand all Black history, including that which is revealed in the Bible. If we are ignorant of our history and its heritage, we will walk blindly into our future, and without keeping in our minds and hearts the spiritual and eternal dimensions of our history, our future forebodes a hopelessness which many of us would rather not face![2] Contrary to the teachings of some European scholars like Frobenius, Africans came to America and to American Christianity with a spiritual conception of God.

OUR AFRICAN CONCEPTION OF GOD

The Yoruba people of West Africa had a very high view of God whom they called *Olïd£marä*. Like Elohim in the Book of Genesis, *Olïd£marä* was the supreme God. The Yoruba's Bible was unwritten. Theirs was an oral tradition, a tradition of memorized scriptures. Just as the Christian Bible has 39 books in the Old Testament and 27 books in the New Testament, the Yoruba *Odu* had 256 books which contained 1,680 stories.

Olïd£marä was the origin and giver of life. He was called *Elemi*, "the owner of the spirit" or "the owner of life." Olïd£mará was all-wise, all-knowing and all-see-ing. Olïd£mará was like God in Psalm 139, the God who sees all we do and hears all we say.[3] Nigerian scholar E. Bolaji Idowu in his book, Olïd£mará, God in Yoruba Belief, says that Yoruba people never sought revenge because they trusted Olïd£mará to pay back people for the evil they did to others.[4] Dr. Anthony Evans says that in America we suffer from a Rambo complex. We feel compelled to pay back evil for evil.[5]

OUR SLAVE TRADITION

Because of their African ethics of non-revenge and their high view of God, our foremothers and forefathers had no trouble embracing the God of American Christianity. They worshiped in the woods in brush harbors or self-made praise houses. They prayed around a pot turned upside down to absorb the sound. To be heard praying and praising God meant that, if caught, they would be beaten. In the fields where they worked, the slaves could be heard singing: "I couldn't hear nobody pray. Way down yonder by myself, I couldn't hear nobody pray." This meant that they were safe because the slave masters could not hear them praising, praying, and preaching. Albert Rabateau tells us about this in Slave Religion. Eugene D. Genovese talks about it in Roll, Jordan, Roll: The World the Slaves Made. You and I owe a great debt of gratitude for the spirituality and prayer tradition of our ances-tors.

Our elders were genuine in praising and praying. In 1920, the Reverend George E. Morris, D.D., from Morristown, New Jersey, wrote The Ante-Bellum Religious Life of the Race. He said of our forebearers:

> "Their religion was their life . . . They sang under all circumstances in meeting houses, in their homes, in the fields, behind the plow, casting forth from the sickle, binding the sheaves, digging trenches, felling forests in hot, in cold, in joy, in sorrow. . . . They lived on prayer. . . . This is what kept up their strong, vigorous faith and gave them such a glorious hope. . . . They were as patient as the earth and the stars above. It was the implicit trust in God, exercised by fervent, believing prayer that kept them from despondency and suicide."[6]

The richness of our foremothers' and forefathers' prayer life should inspire us to recover and rediscover the importance of prayer for our survival and for our social transformation.

THE RECOVERY OF OUR AFRICAN AMERICAN PRAYER TRADITION

If prayer fueled the faith of our elders, if faith enabled them to rise against adversity, if prayer gave them strength to overcome all adversities, why should we reinvent the wheel? Why should we discard that which works? Why can't our personal and collective lives be empowered by our renewed emphasis on prayer?

Do you not agree that for too long we have been a dependent people? For too long we have depended upon government programs, government student loans, and government subsidies and entitlement programs to see us through. Yes, I know that we pay taxes; therefore, we should enjoy the benefits of our citizenship. Yes, I know that for too long, justice has been denied the poor and the powerless. I know that for too long those who have had the least have paid the most to feed the unsatisfied appetite of a greedy military war machine. But I know that our predecessors had no friends but themselves and God Almighty. They had no civil rights. They had no constitutional protection. They had disenfranchisement, poll tax, literary tests, gerrymandering, redlining, exclusion from history books; they had segregation in the military, in public transportation, and public accommodations. But their dependency was on the God of their weary years and the God of their silent tears.

Their dependency when hope unborn had died was in Jesus Christ. He came into their sick rooms as a doctor, as a psychiatrist; He was a heart-fixer and a mind-regulator. He was a lawyer in the courtroom. Jesus was a friend to the friendless, a husband to the widow, a mother to the motherless, and a father to the fatherless.

CONCLUSION

Our African ancestors gave thanks to the Lord. They proclaimed His greatness—told the nations what God had done for them. They sang praises to the Lord. They sang through their crises. They had power to triumph. They were victors over tragedy, not victims of depression, oppression, and suppression. As our Scripture text reminds us, they went to the Lord for help. But once the Lord helped them, they never strayed. Hear them as they prayed:

I want Jesus to walk with me,

I want Jesus to walk with me.

All along my pilgrim journey,

I want Jesus to walk with me.[7]

BIBLE STUDY APPLICATION

INSTRUCTIONS: The following exercises provide the opportunity to study more closely, points made by Dr. Smith in this chapter. The Bible contains prayers that are a part of the prayer tradition of Black people. The biblical references are based on both the *King James Version* and the *Good News Bible*.

1. Hagar

Hagar was an African who was a servant of Abraham and Sarah. She is an ancestor of Africans and African Americans whose prayers are a part of the prayer tradition of Black people.

a. From what country was Hagar? (Genesis 25:12)

b. Ham means "burnt skin," "hot," or "heat" in Hebrew. Ham is considered the father of African people. What are the "lands of Ham" that became Egypt? (10:13-14) In all likelihood, what was the race of Hagar?

c. How did Hagar come to bear a child to Abraham? (16:1-4)

d. Under what circumstances did Hagar pray? (16:1-16) How did this prayer change Hagar's relationship with God?

e. Under what circumstances was it that Hagar had another conversation with God? (21:1-19) What was her prayer? (21:16) What difference did this encounter with God have on her life? (21:19-21, read the story between the lines)

Summary Question: Considering your answers to a-e above, what comparisons can be made between Hagar and single African American parents today? What can you learn from Hagar's situation about prayer? In what sense are Hagar's prayers a part of the prayer tradition of Black people?

2. Job

The story of Job is cast in an African setting. In all likelihood, Job would be considered an ancestor of African Americans. Therefore, the prayers of Job fit into the prayer tradition of African people.

a. Who was Job? (Job 1:1-5) What happened to him? (1:6-19)

b. From what country was Job? (1:1) To what ancestors can the people of the Uz be traced? (Genesis 10:21-23)

c. To whom were the ancestors of the people of Uz related? (10:1)

Ham is considered the ancestor of people who populated Africa. What evidence is there of intermarriage between Shemites and Hamites? (1 Chronicles 1:28, 34; Genesis 10:6; 36:1-4) What was the likely race of the people of Uz? Explain your answers.

d. In what circumstance did Job first pray? (Job 1:13-20) In what circumstances did Job's second prayer occur? (2:1—3:26)

e. What was Job's final prayer? (Job 42:1-6)

Summary Question: Consider your answers to a-e above. On what basis can Job's situation be compared to those of many African Americans today? In what sense are Job's prayers part of the prayer tradition of African Americans? What can you learn from Job about prayer?

3. Hannah

Hannah's prayer also belongs to the prayer tradition of African Americans and Africans.

a. Who was Hannah? From what country was she? (1 Samuel 1:1-2) Who were the father and mother of the Ephraimites? (Genesis 41:50-52)

b. From what country was Asenath, Ephraim's mother? (41:44-45) Who was the father of Mizraim, or Egypt? (10:6) What was the likely race of Hannah?

c. What circumstances surrounded Hannah's first prayer? (1 Samuel 1:1-13) What was the outcome of her prayer? (1:19-20)

d. What was the circumstance surrounding Hannah's second prayer? (1:21-28)

e. Considering your answers to a-d above, what is the meaning of some of the references in Hannah's prayer? (1 Samuel 2:1-10) What famous prayer might Hannah have inspired? (Luke 1:46-55)

Summary Question: Considering your answers to a-e above, what comparisons can be made between the situation of Hannah and those of many African Americans today? What can you learn from Hannah's situation about prayer?

4. Paul

The Apostle Paul's prayers can be considered among those in the prayer tradition of Black people.

a. From what tribe was Paul? (Romans 11:1) To whom can Benjamin be traced? (Genesis 35:16-18; 25:1-26; 17:19; 11:10-31)

b. How did the Jews connect the tribe of Benjamin to the first human beings? (9:18) Where were the first humans created? (2:1-22) What was the likely race of Paul?

c. What were the circumstances surrounding one of Paul's (Saul's) prayers? (Acts 9:1-5) What was the outcome of this prayer? (9:7-19)

d. What were the circumstances surrounding another of Paul's prayers?

(Acts 16:16-25) What was the outcome? (16:26-40)

e. What are some other situations in which Paul prayed, and what were the outcomes? (27:23-44)

Summary Question: Considering your answers to a-e above, what can you learn from Paul's life about prayer? How are Paul's prayers a part of the tradition of Black people?

5. The Syro-Phoenician Woman

The prayer of the Syro-Phoenician woman can be added to the prayer tradition of Black people.

a. From what geographical area was the Syro-Phoenician woman? (Matthew 15:21-22) To what ancestors can Phoenicians (Sidonians) be traced? (Genesis 10:15; 10:6)

b. To whom can the ancestors of Canaan be traced? (Genesis 10:6) What was the likely race of this woman?

c. What relationship had existed between the Canaanites and the Jews? (Judges 3:5-6; Genesis 28:1, 6; 36:1-5)

d. What was the circumstance surrounding this woman's prayer? (Matthew 15:21-23)

e. What caused the Syro-Phoenician woman to persist in prayer? What was the outcome of her persistence? (15:28)

Summary Question: What similarities are there between the situation of the Syro-Phoenician woman and those of many African Americans today? What can you learn from the Syro-Phoenician woman about prayer?

6. Ministry Application

Identify a person in your congregation who is a known prayer-warrior. Write a short story about that person's testimony and share it with the children at your church. Be sure to explain how this praying person is a part of the prayer tradition of Black people.

7. Personal Application

Identify the most important insight that you gained from the study of the prayer lives of Hagar, Job, Hannah, Paul, and the Syro-Phoenician woman. How can this insight improve your prayer life?

From the Pastor's Pen

Many give up on prayer after not receiving that for which they prayed. Does that mean that prayer is a hoax? Does this mean that God is capricious or a promise breaker? Does this mean that an uncaring God refuses to compassionately heal the praying person in the last stages of cancer? What does it mean to ask God for anything in the name of Jesus? Does it mean that the Gospel of John is giving inaccurate information on the correct formula for having a yes answer to prayer?

"Name" means the person or the nature and spirit of a person. A name must harmonize with the Spirit of Jesus, with the will of God. So Jesus is saying, "Ask anything that is pleasing to the Father and what is good for you, and I will do it."[1]

You and I cannot receive what will harm us from the hands of a loving and caring heavenly Parent. God is always true to the spiritual consistency law that operates for your and my best interests. Sometimes God's no is the best answer to our prayers. Human finiteness cannot unravel the mysteries of the infinite God. Keep praying.

CHAPTER NINE

HOW FAR WILL YOUR PRAYERS TAKE YOU?

"Then they that gladly received his word were baptized: and the same day there were added unto them about three thousand souls. And they continued stedfastly in the apostles' doctrine and fellowship, . . . and in prayers . . . and many wonders and signs were done . . . And all that believed were together, and had all things common; And sold their possessions . . . and parted them . . . as every man had need. And they, continuing daily with one accord . . . Praising God, and having favour with all the people. And the Lord added to the church daily such as should be saved"
(Acts 2:41-47, KJV).

INTRODUCTION

How much mileage does your car give you per gallon of gasoline? How far down the road does each gallon of gasoline take you? If your mileage is poor, perhaps it is because your motor needs overhauling, or because your gasoline is of a cheap quality, or your driving habits are poor. In an inflationary age when prices continue to go upward and wages do not increase with the cost of living, you and I should seek better gasoline mileage with our hard earned dollars.

If you and I need to practice discipline and restraint in economics in order to get maximum value for our dollars, is it not also true that in the spiritual world you and I should receive maximum mileage from our prayers? How far will your prayers take you?

A PERSONAL INVENTORY

Why are you here today? Have you come for a spiritual check-up? Some want a spiritual tune-up without having a spiritual check-up. A tune-up that overlooks the check-up is a cover-up of what is wrong. What is the state of your soul?

Spiritually, are you a dusty and desolate desert, or a frozen field barren with snow? Is your soul a fragile and skinny tree with shallow roots struggling to survive the fierce winds of life? Or is your soul a weakly constructed house whose faulty foundation rests on a feared earthquake fault?

How far will your prayers take you? Is your prayer life like an automobile that causes danger to countless rush hour freeway travelers, because you dared to drive home from work on the fumes from an empty gasoline tank? Is your prayer life like a bank account that has been overdrawn? Does God refuse to give a "yes" answer to your prayers because your prayer account has insufficient funds? Is your soul starved and thirsty even after you hear good preaching and singing, because you are like a careless farmer depending upon government subsidies to help you survive the cold winds of winter and the flood waters of a wet spring?

What is the state of your prayer life? How far will your prayers take you? Has your telephone of prayer been temporarily disconnected or permanently disconnected because of the non-payment of your spiritual discipline? Is the static on your prayer telephone interfering with your communications with God? Why do you allow the world's static to prevent you from having a clear and open line of communication with God? Is your comprehension of God's message to you on the telephone of prayer clear enough to take you to serious commitment and loyal obedience to God's will? Will your prayers take you past a cold, artificial experience to a genuine intimacy with God?

How far will your prayers take you? Will your prayers take you from spiritual disease to spiritual health? Are your blood vessels free from the viruses of bitterness and revenge? Is your heart strong enough to love the unlovable who hate and harm you? Is your spirit gentle enough for you to be compassionate to the underclass and the unemployed whose low self-esteem make them feel unworthy of belonging to any of the churches in town? Are your legs tough enough to pick yourself up off the ground after you have slipped or been knocked down by toughness, trials, or tribulations? How far will your prayers take you?

How far should your prayers take you? Someone answered by saying:

"I may have doubts and fears, my eye be filled with tears, but Jesus is a friend who watches day and night; I go to Him in prayer, He knows my every care, and just a little talk with Jesus makes it right."[2]

Our Scripture text clarifies the matter. The text says,
"And they continued stedfastly in the apostles' doctrine and fellow-

ship, and in breaking of bread, and in prayers"
(Acts 2:42, KJV).

CONTINUING STEADFASTLY

This text is a challenge to each of us. The text calls you and me to settle down in one church where we can grow spiritually. Jesus, our spiritual coach, seeks champions who will not only start out in a church but who will have staying power. Spiritual dropouts and church tramps do not continue "stedfastly in the apostles' doctrine and fellowship, and in breaking of bread, and in prayers" (Acts 2:42, KJV).

Immature church members are weak persons who are spiritually infatuated with the latest spiritual fad that comes to town. These church members with weak convictions are an easy prey for any popular preacher, cult, or church with a large following. They join a church without ever beginning to become disciples tutored by the pastor. They are fringe members who never engage in the painful and slow discipline that produces, in time, informed Christians who enrich their lives with productive prayer. These lukewarm church members are unprepared for surviving the trials and tribulations of stormy weather. The slippery sleet and snow of winter and the sickening heat of summer overcome them, and they end up blaming the church for their inability to face life with victorious faith. They soon become absentee church members who fall by the wayside with the cynical and defeated. How far you and I travel on the rough roads of life depends upon our personal discipline and dedication. You and I cannot blame the preacher, deacon, choir, or church for our failures. You and I must determine for ourselves how far our prayers will take us.

The Greek word for "continued steadfastly" must become our personal possession. That word is *proskarterountes*. It means to continue, persevere, endure, stick, or persist. A disciplined disciple does not quit, back off, fade away, or slip back. A disciplined prayer life helps you and me to continue steadfastly in the apostles' teaching and in the mission of Jesus Christ. How far will your prayers take you?

High octane prayer will give you power to speed up high mountains and to carry heavy burdens across the never ending valleys. High octane prayer will ignite the spark plugs of faith to start the motor of conviction on any cold morning of frozen enthusiasm. High octane prayer will help you to continue even unto the last mile of life's journey. Others may give up and quit, but high octane prayer will enable you to finish the race with the sound of "Well done, good and faithful servant."[3]

How far will your prayers take you? Consistency in prayer will help you to continue steadfastly.

CONCLUSION

Continue steadfastly in being faithful in your promises to God. Continue steadfastly in being firm in God's purposes. Continue steadfastly in being fearless in God's principles, and continue steadfastly in being fervent in your prayers.

I challenge you to a spiritual life of consistency and continuity. I call you to a steadfast and sturdy devotional life of praise and prayer. I charge you to narrow your focus to a Christ-centered focus. I ask you to commit yourself to personal spiritual improvement.

BIBLE STUDY APPLICATION

INSTRUCTIONS: The following exercises provide the opportunity to study more closely, points raised by Dr. Smith in this chapter. The biblical references are based on both the *King James Version* and the *Good News Bible*.

1. Asking

Dr. Smith says that we must continue steadfastly in prayer. One of the components of prayer is asking God for what we want and need.

a. What is the promise of God for those who ask God? (Matthew 7:7, 9-11; 1 John 5:14)

b. When we ask God, what attitude is essential? (Matthew 21:18-22)

c. When we ask God, what else is essential? (John 15:1-7)

d. What interferes with our willingness to ask God? (James 1:2-8; 4:1-3)

e. Is the outcome of prayers limited to what we can see? Explain your answer. (Ephesians 3:20-21)

Summary Question: How do your answers to a-e above apply to your prayer life?

2. Prayers in the New Testament

The New Testament Gospels contain numerous examples of people who communicated with Jesus as Jesus carried out His earthly ministry.

a. What was the circumstance of the man who asked Jesus to make him clean? (Matthew 8:1-2; Leviticus 13:2-2, 45-46) How far did his prayers take him? (Matthew 8:3-4)

b. What was the circumstance of the woman who reached out to Jesus? (Mark 5:25-26; Leviticus 15:25-33) How far did her prayers take her? (Mark 5:27-34)

c. What was the circumstance of the disciples who sought Jesus' help? (Luke 8:22-23) How far did their prayer take them? (8:24-25)

d. What was the circumstance of Thomas when he cried out to the Lord? (John 20:19-28) How far did his communication with God take him? (Acts 1:1—2:4)

e. What was the circumstance of the disciples who assisted Jesus in His earthly ministry? (Matthew 14:15-17) What was their request? How did Jesus respond to their communication? (14:15-19) How far did this conversation with Jesus take them?

Summary Question: Based on your answers to a-e above, how far can prayer take a person? What are similarities and differences between these historical people and people today? What can you learn from these short stories about prayer?

3. Prayer While Ministering

Dr. Smith says that prayer can take a person a long way in the course of ministry.

a. What was the predicament of Dorcas when Peter encountered her? (Acts 9:36-37) How far did Peter's prayer take him? (9:40-42)

b. How far did the prayers of the leaders at Antioch take them, where they ordained Paul for the ministry? (13:1-12)

c. How far did the prayers of the leaders at Antioch take them in preparing Paul to evangelize the Gentiles? (13:3-4, 14-16, 42-49)

d. What challenge faced Paul in carrying out his ministry at Philippi? (16:12, 16-24) How far did Paul and Silas' prayers take them? (16:25-34)

e. What was another challenge facing the apostles in the early church? (6:1-2) How far did their prayers take them? (6:3-7)

Summary Question: Considering your answers to a-e, how far can prayer take a Christian while encountering daily challenges of ministry? What can you learn from these short stories about prayer and how can you apply it to your prayer life?

4. Answered Prayers in the Old Testament

The Old Testament contains numerous examples of answered prayer.

a. How far did one of Elijah's prayers take him? (1 Kings 18:16-40)

b. How far did the prayer of Elisha take him? (2 Kings 6:8-23)

c. How far did Nehemiah's prayers take him? (Nehemiah 1:1--2:6; 6:15-16)

d. What predicament faced Daniel? (Daniel 6:1-17) How far did his prayers take him? (6:10, 21-28)

e. What predicament did Hezekiah inherit as king? (2 Chronicles 28:22-27) What did Hezekiah set out to do? (29:3-8, 10; 27—31:1, 20-21)

Summary Question: Compare and contrast the challenges faced by the people mentioned in a-e above. What can you learn from their stories about the power of prayer?

5. Promised Outcomes of Prayer

God is committed to answering prayers.

a. What promise is there for the afflicted? (Psalm 22:24)

b. What promise is there for those who take their burdens to the Lord? (55:22)

c. What promise is there for those who come to the Lord? (Matthew 11:28)

d. What is God's promise to those who sing praises unto the Lord? (Psalm 27:5, 6)

e. What promise is there for those who abide in Christ? (John 15)

Summary Question: Meditate for a moment, after asking the Lord to remind you of a particular prayer at an important moment of your life. How far did your prayer take you? Which of God's promises were fulfilled? Share your story with someone this week.

6. Ministry Application

Design a testimony time for your church's weekday Bible study or prayer meeting. Invite people to share outcomes of their prayers. Name the event, "How Far Did Your Prayers Take You?" Allow for time of singing and praising the Lord.

7. Personal Application

What is one major point, made by Dr. Smith in this chapter, which applies to your life? How will you use the insights to improve your prayer life?

From the Pastor's Pen

The Greeks were educated in order to understand the Hebrews of the Jewish Bible (Old Testament). The Hebrews were educated in order to revere or honor the Creator of creation. The Romans were educated to have the power to control nature and barbarians whom they considered to be "the lesser breeds of the human race." The modern world is educated to succeed in the competitive race to gain material wealth.

Jesus taught Christian disciples to become educated in order to serve and help make human life more humane. The modern university teaches information and neglects the tutoring and coaching of the soul. Hence, many educated people are self-centered, greedy, and Godless.

The tutoring of the soul comes from the daily discipline of prayer. Prayer tames our meanness and turns us into gentle, loving, caring, and compassionate persons who love beauty, holiness, and truth. Prayer transforms us from animals who destroy each other with words and deeds into disciples of the Master Teacher who refuse to cooperate with evil. Educated Christians, made mellow by prayer, ask not, What will I take from life, but what will life get out of me? The world is in short supply of educated disciples who "love mercy, do justly, and walk humbly with God" in paths of righteous service. Let us pray for disciples who through prayerful study are tutored by the Master Teacher.

Maturity in prayer helps us to grow beyond pestering God about our self-centered agenda for health and wealth. The health and wealth evangelists on television preach a gospel of prosperity and materialism and not the Gospel of Jesus Christ, who was a person for others. As you and I study the prayer life of Jesus, we will not be able to avoid noticing how Jesus refused to be a whimpering, demanding, spiritual baby, who demanded that God cater to His every need. An anonymous scholar says it best in Cecil Osborne's The Art of Understanding Yourself:

Saints are persons who permit God's forgiveness
to come into them so fully that not only
are their sins washed out, but also their very selves,
their egos, and the root of their self will . . . .
I forgive to the level that I have been forgiven,

*and if that level is moderate because I wanted to lose
my vices and not myself, I can forgive only people
who have offended moderately, and my forgiveness
helps them only moderately.*[1]

*Mature prayer challenges us to go all of the way in unselfishness and in for-
giveness. Mature prayer moves us to examine our motives daily and to dig
deeply into our hearts to uproot hidden motives of pretense, pride, and self-
justification so that God's forgiveness may come to us fully. May God help us
to mature fully in our prayer life.*

CHAPTER TEN

PRAYER FOR THE REWRITING OF BLACK HISTORY

"Princes shall come out of Egypt; Ethiopia shall soon stretch out her hands unto God"

(Psalm 68:31, KJV)

INTRODUCTION

As early as my boyhood days, this verse posed a problem for me. Growing up in segregated Missouri, where I could not eat in restaurants, sleep in hotels, ride in integrated railway coaches, attend integrated schools, or witness integrated athletic contests, my painful anger would lash out at God. I would say: "Grandmother, God is not fair. If God were just as you say, God would destroy segregation and racial prejudice." Grandmother would always respond to my hurt by quoting the *King James Version* of Psalm 68:31, "Princes shall come out of Egypt; Ethiopia shall soon stretch out her hands unto God." Although I believed in God's presence and power, I was an agnostic where God's purpose was concerned. The text just didn't make any sense to me. God, who has power to change things, is not doing much to improve life for Africans or African Americans. As a child, my teachers told me that Africa was "the dark continent." Christian missionaries told me that Africans were war-like savages who captured white men, only to cut off their heads. The movies taught me that Africans were naked, backward people, fearful of lions, tigers, and crocodiles, and that only tall blonde and blue-eyed Tarzan could tame apes, swim faster than crocodiles, and ride elephants. I grew up in an era when Black boys and men were lynched by mobs who saw Blacks as persons cursed by God with either "the mark of Cain," or "the curse of Noah upon Canaan." I thought that my saintly grandmother was well-meaning, but foolishly misled in quoting to me our text: "Princes shall come out of Egypt." Egypt was the land of oppression.

Ethiopia was raped and ruined in my boyhood days by Mussolini and the Italian Army. Could not my grandmother find another text to offer me?

Yet, I stand before you, in holy boldness, offering you what I rejected from the lips and soul of my grandmother. "Ambassadors will come from Egypt; the Sudanese will raise their hands in prayer to God" (Psalm 68:31, TEV).

OUR TEXT'S HISTORY

Cain Hope Felder in *Troubling Biblical Waters* laments the patronizing and negative bais of Western biblical scholars toward Scriptures which mention Egypt and Ethiopia. He speaks unhappily of the scant attention they have paid to the origin and development of Christianity in Ethiopia.[2] These scholars had not read Cheikh Anta Diop's *The African Origins of Civilization*[3] or Charles Copher's *The Black Man in the Biblical World*. Neither had my untutored grandmother read these books, yet she quoted to me again and again: "Princes shall come out of Egypt; Ethiopia shall soon stretch out her hands to God."

According to scholars Walter McCray, Charles Copher, Randall Bailey, and Cain Hope Felder, Genesis 10 describes the table of nations. According to this genealogical table, Noah's son, Ham, gave birth to the African peoples of Cush, Mizraim, Phut or Put, and Canaan. Cush, which means "black" in Hebrew, was the land of Ethiopia. Mizraim was the land of Egypt, which was called Chem by the Egyptians. Phut or Put was representative of Cyrene or Libya.

Canaan represented what is now known as Palestine, Lebanon, Jordan, and North Africa. Remember Moses in Egypt marrying a Black woman? Phinehas in Moses' family was a Nubian or Negro. The term "Phinehas" means "Negro." Joseph, before Moses, married an Egyptian woman named Asenath, and they had two sons born in Africa. These Africans were Ephraim and Manasseh. From 922 to 722 B.C.E., the biblical world experienced a powerful Black presence. During Amos' time, the Ethiopians were known as a people of renown. Second Kings 17:4 reports that King Hoshea sent messengers to Egypt for military assistance. Around 714 B.C.E., during the time of the Prophet Isaiah, both Ethiopia and Egypt were looked up to by Judah, who needed these Black nations to protect her from the Assyrians under King Sargon II.

Oh, what a glorious recital of past Black history. How grand! How noble! How admirable! How wonderful it is to know that the brilliant and rich Queen of Sheba was Black and beautiful! However, we cannot live in the golden age of beautiful Black biblical history.

THE TEXT IN TODAY'S WORLD

Psalm 68:31 is a call to action. This verse is an alarm sounded to wake up a people lost in the wilderness of the 20th and 21st centuries. How long will we wander in the wilderness of complacency?

What do we see from our pedestal of self-scrutiny? What is our present history? Is it one of lost pride, weak-willed purpose, and moral decadence? Or is our present one where Blacks have the faith of the world and are not feared by the world? Are youthful, trained ambassadors emerging from Black roots to bless the world with mental and moral richness, or does the world find itself seeing Africans and African Americans as problems, rather than people with problems? Does the rest of the people of God's rainbow feel led to ignore us, destroy us, or paternalistically stop us from either starving each other or killing each other in combat zones where Blacks have declared Black life is cheap?

Let us rewrite our history. Let new ambassadors, both women and men, come forth from Egypt with promise and productivity. Let us rewrite our history by repairing our damaged dignity, with manuscripts of mental excellence and moral elegance. Let us rewrite our history by renewing our self-esteem that was ripped by racism's razor. Let us, who know God, rewrite our history. Let us rewrite our history by blessing the rainbow-colored races of God's family with blessings in black, as did our foremothers and -fathers. Let us, who love God, rewrite our history. Let us rewrite our history by rebuilding Black family life on confession, forgiveness, unity, and unconditional love. Let us remember those who are to follow us and rewrite a better future for them. Let us rewrite our history by never turning back, but moving ever forward with our eyes on the prize.

CONCLUSION

Let us, the new Sudanese, raise our hands in prayer to God. If we would climb mountains, cross deserts, conquer enemies, we must not forget to raise our hands in prayer to God. If we would form character in our children, reform our deformed institutions, inform the uninformed in society, perform as partners participating in kingdom building, and be transformed by the power of the Holy Spirit, we must raise our hands in prayer to God.

God will not forget us. Even in our grave God will not leave us in the dust. God will resurrect us and our works into the eternal dimensions of history, even as God raised Jesus from the dead.

BIBLE STUDY APPLICATION

INSTRUCTIONS: The following exercises provide the opportunity to examine more closely, the points raised by Dr. Smith in this chapter. The biblical references are based on both the *King James Version* of the Bible and the *Good News Bible*.

1. Recorders of God's Victories

In ancient Israel, God called writers frequently to record the history of God's victories for the benefit of future generations.

a. Who is one biblical leader whom God commissioned to write a segment of Israel's history? (Exodus 17:4) What was the event that God called Moses to record? (17:8-14)

b. Within what context had the Amalekites attacked Israel? (14:19-21; 16:4-5;13:11-16; 17:1-7)

c. Why did God ask Moses to record this victory? (17:14-16)

d. What type relationship would exist between the Israelites and the Amalekites in future generations? (Deuteronomy 25:17-19; Judges 3:12-14; 6:3-6; 7:1, 12; 8:28)

e. Eventually, what happened to the Amalekites? (1 Samuel 14:47-48; 15:4-9; 27:8-11; 30:1-2, 18; 1 Chronicles 4:41-43)

Summary Question: It appears that the struggle between Israel and the Amalekites lasted for centuries. However, God had asked Moses to record God's victory over them for the benefit of future generations. Why was this written record of victory important? (Numbers 24:20) What parallels can be drawn between the Israelite situation and people of African descent in various parts of the world today? Why are writers important within this modern context?

2. Recorders of the Prophets

Prophets in ancient Israel were busy people, without time to write. Sometimes they hired writers to serve under them.

a. What is the name of one writer who served under the Prophet Jeremiah? (Jeremiah 36:4) What was Baruch's family background? (2 Chronicles 34:8-13; Jeremiah 32:12; 51:59)

b. What were some of Baruch's responsibilities? (32:11-15; 36:4, 10-18)

c. What happened to Baruch as a result of his affiliation with Jeremiah? (43:1-7)

d. About what types of issues did Baruch write, under the direction of Jeremiah? (36:1-8; 45—51)

e. Baruch is said to have written a collection of essays that are considered by Protestants as a part of the *Apocrypha*. What are they?

Summary Question: Who are some of the great "prophets" among African Americans today? Is there a need to record the teachings of God that come through them? Where might the African American community locate the "Baruchs" of today? How far-reaching was Baruch's work?

3. Recorders of the History of a People

Sometimes God called writers to record the history of Israel so that future generations could learn by both the mistakes and victories of Israelites.

a. What were two major works of the Prophet Isaiah? (2 Chronicles 26:22; 32:32)

b. What were some of the accomplishments of Uzziah? (2 Kings 14:21-22; 2 Chronicles 26:1-14)

c. What mistakes did Uzziah make? (26:16-21; Numbers 16:40; 18:7)

d. What impact did Uzziah's life have? (2 Chronicles 26:23—27:2)

e. Why did Isaiah feel it was important to record the events of Uzziah's life along with other events in the history of Israel? (Isaiah 30:8-18)

Summary Question: Considering your answers to a-e above, why is it important to keep a record of mistakes as well as victories of African Americans' struggles against oppression? What are some mistakes we have made in the past? What are mistakes we are making today? How might the recording of these mistakes and victories help future generations?

4. Investigative Reporters

In some instances, God called writers to collect and organize stories to be examined by future generations. Sometimes He called these same reporters to record their personal eyewitness reports.

a. Who was Luke, the author of the Books of Luke and Acts? (Colossians 4:14)

b. How did Luke go about gathering information he wrote about in the Gospel of Luke? (Luke 1:1-4)

c. How might he have gathered information used to write about many of the events presented in the Book of Acts? (Acts 1:1-10)

d. Of which events in Paul's life was Luke an eyewitness? (16:10-17) Of what other events in Paul's life was Luke an eyewitness? (20:6—21:18)

e. How did Luke gain information about Paul's imprisonment? (21:27; 27:1-12; 28:20)

Summary Question: Considering your answers to a-e above, can you draw parallels between the role that Luke played in the first century after Christ with the role that African American Christian writers play today? In what sense is there a need for more "Lukes" today?

5. Inspirational Writers

In some cases God called people to write the type of inspirational literature that would cause Christians to move forward in their spiritual lives.

a. Who was James, author of the Epistle of James? (Matthew 13:53-56; Mark 6:3)

b. What was James' original attitude toward Jesus' ministry? (John 7:1-5)

c. What might have changed James' opinion concerning who Jesus was? (1 Corinthians 15:5, 7; Acts 1:12-14; 2:1-4, 43-47)

d. How did James develop the insights that he used to write the Epistle of James? (Galatians 1:1-2, 15-19; 2:8-10; Acts 21:17-19)

e. What is the primary topic of the Epistle of James? (James 1:1-8)

Summary Question: Is there a need for writers to develop inspirational literature for African Americans today? What guidelines can be learned from the Epistle of James?

6. Ministry Application

Are there potential writers among members of your church? What are some strategies for encouraging them to use their gifts and interests for the Lord?

7. Personal Application

Have you ever thought of becoming a writer? What are the first steps that you can take?

From the Pastor's Pen

The famous scientist, Doctor George Washington Carver, was a person of prayer. He is a classic example of African American spirituality. At Tuskegee where he taught science and a volunteer extra curricular Bible class, Dr. Carver is reported by former student Alvin D. Smith to have said:

"Contact thy Creator, learn how to tune in with Him, and He will——through you—work miracles. He will guide you to peace, happiness, prosperity—to all your heart's desires."

Let's meet each Thursday for prayer, for meeting God in a fresh encounter of Divine—human communion.

CHAPTER ELEVEN

SUCCESS AND FAILURE IN PRAYER

*"And he spake this parable unto certain which trusted in themselves
that they were righteous, and despised others: Two men went up into
the temple to pray; the one a Pharisee, and the other a publican. The
Pharisee . . . prayed thus . . . God, I thank thee, that I am not as other
men are . . . I fast . . . I give tithes . . . And the publican . . . would not
lift . . . his eyes unto heaven, . . . saying, God be merciful to me a sinner. I tell you, this man went down to his house justified rather than
the other; for every one who exalteth himself shall be abased; and he
that humbleth himself shall be exalted"*
(Luke 18:9-14, KJV).

INTRODUCTION

Not all prayers are successful. Some prayers fail to be answered by God. A fax service, run by Bezek, the Israeli national phone company, enables Jews to fax prayers to them from anywhere in the world. Bezek employees then take these prayers to the Wailing Wall in Jerusalem and place the prayers in the crevices of the wall. Such action is bound to fail. God is not interested in paper prayers. Our God seeks the prayers of a sincere heart. Prayers couched in elegant language may be pleasing to the ear, but God is not impressed with grammar, style, prose or poetry when hearing us pray. Repetitious phrases fail to claim God's attention. The loudness of the voice in praying does not impress God more than a silent prayer that emanates from a sincere heart. The number of candles burned on an altar do not increase a person's chances of being in the favor of God. The sweet fragrance of incense burning at a prayer altar or the use of prayer cloth cannot insure the success of a prayer being heard by God.

Prayers that are successful are prayed in utter humility and simplicity. Jesus wanted persons to pray meaningful prayers. This is why He told a story about success and failure in prayer. In this story He describes the prayer styles of a Pharisee and a publican.

THE PHARISEE'S PRAYER

In Jewish society, Pharisees were deeply religious people. They were very strict and disciplined in the observance of high moral and ethical codes. No religious group worked as hard as the Pharisees in being clean and righteous. The Pharisees avoided sinners. They strove to be clean in an unclean world. Very few Christians in today's world could measure up to the Pharisee's high levels of righteousness. Very few church members are as serious about integrity and honesty as were the Pharisees. In fact, Pharisees were as nearly perfect as it is possible for people to become. Pharisees were the saints of Jesus' day. Yet, Jesus informs us of a Pharisee who was unsuccessful in his prayer life.

A Pharisee arrived for his daily prayer at the same time as a tax collector. The setting was the great, beautiful temple of Herod. The time was either 9:00 a.m. or 3:00 p.m., the official hours of prayer. Picture these two men coming to the temple. Two men going in the right direction. Two men going to the right place. Two men going to do the right thing. Two men of different backgrounds. The Pharisee was religious. The publican was notoriously unreligous by reputation.

Both men were separated from each other in the temple. They had no contact or communion with each other. Each one ignored the other in their efforts to have contact and communion with God. Both men prayed. But both men prayed different prayers.

THE PHARISEE PRAYED A PRAYER OF THANKSGIVING

"God, I thank thee, that I am not as other men are, extortioners, unjust, adulterers, or even as this publican. I fast twice in the week, I give tithes of all that I possess"
(Luke 18:11-12, KJV).

Hear him praying out loud so all could hear him. Hear him brag or boast about himself before God. Look at me, God. Look at me, people. See what a good man I am. God, look at me. I am saved and sanctified, living free from sin all day. You should be proud of me. Look at my accomplishments. I deserve Your blessings. The tax collectors, robbers, adulterers, and evildoers deserve Your wrath and punishment. Destroy them, so that we Pharisees can live in a society free from crime. God, what is that tax collector doing here in Your holy house? He and his kind should not be welcome here. Do something, God. Make Your holy house clean again. Rid Your holy place of tax collectors and other sinners. God, I didn't come here to beg You. I just came here to thank You. I know You will accept this prayer. I fast twice a week when Your law says once a year is enough. God, didn't You read about this in Leviticus 16:29? Don't You read Your Book, God?

God, I give more to this temple than anybody. Some obey Numbers 18:21 and give the Levitic tithe. They also obey Deuteronomy 14:28 and give the poor man's tithe. They obey Deuteronomy 14:22 and give the Jerusalem tithe. But Lord, did You hear me, I give a tithe of all that I possess.

THE TAX COLLECTOR'S PRAYER

The poor, guilty tax collector was ashamed and embarrassed by his sin. He knew that he did not deserve God's mercy and forgiveness. So he kept his distance. He stood far off. He could not raise his head and look at the altar. He was disappointed with himself. He became emotional; he hit himself on the chest again and again, and he cried out:

"God be merciful to me a sinner"
(Luke 18:13, KJV).

The sinner cried for mercy. He said, please God, remove Your anger. Remove Your judgment. I know that I don't deserve Your love. But I want to be reconciled with You. I need Your forgiveness, I need Your love. I will not have peace until You accept me.

"The sacrifices of God are a broken spirit: a broken and a contrite heart, O God, thou wilt not despise"
(Psalm 51:17, KJV).

"Who is a God like unto thee, that pardoneth iniquity and passeth by the transgression of the remnant of his heritage? he retaineth not his anger for ever, because he delighteth in mercy"
(Micah 7:18, KJV).

Jesus shocked everyone. The Pharisee knew that he was good enough. The tax collector knew that he was bad enough. But the Pharisee forgot to read Proverbs 28:26 (KJV):

> *"He that trusteth in his own heart is a fool: but whoso walketh wisely, he shall be delivered."*

He forgot to read Proverbs 28:13-14 (KJV):

> *"He that covereth his sins shall not prosper: but whoso confesseth and forsaketh them shall have mercy."*

So Jesus shocked everyone. Jesus said that the tax collector went home with a blessing, whereas the Pharisee went home with God's disfavor. Whom does God hear? Whose prayer does God honor? God honors the humble. God saves sinners. God hears the prayer of the one who says:

Just as I am without one plea, but that Thy blood was shed for me,
And that Thou bidd'st me come to Thee,
O Lamb of God, I come! I come!

Just as I am Thou wilt receive,
Wilt welcome, pardon, cleanse, relieve, Because Thy promise I believe,
O Lamb of God, I come! I come![1]

CONCLUSION

You may know someone who is unchurched because he or she does not feel good enough to be a member. You may be an unsaved person, guilty of sin, and troubled in your conscience. Remember, Jesus saves sinners. You may not like the word "sinners." But sin is pride. Sin is saying that I don't need God. Sin is saying that my life as it is, all right. Sin is rebellion against God's Word. Sin is the refusal to care enough to confess your sins to God. Sin is the denial of your condition. Sin is the refusal to change your conduct, to confess, and to trust God.

Does God hear the prayer of a sinner?
The answer is yes.

Just as I am, tho tossed about
With many a conflict, many a doubt,

Fightings and fears within, without,
O Lamb of God, I come! I come!

Just as I am, Thou wilt receive,
Wilt welcome, pardon, cleanse, relieve, because of Thy promise, I believe
O Lamb of God, I come! I come![2]

BIBLE STUDY APPLICATION

INSTRUCTIONS: The following exercises provide the opportunity to study more closely points raised in this chapter. The biblical references are based on both the *King James Version* of the Bible and the *Good News Bible*.

1. Prayers of the Heart
Scripture contains images of people rendered speechless by the pain of their situations, but whose silent prayer reached the heart of God.
a. What might have been the prayer of Rizpah, if her heart could have spoken? (2 Samuel 21:1-10) How did God answer her silent cry? (21:11-14)
b. What might have been the prayer of Ishmael, if his tears could have talked? (Genesis 21:8-17) What might have been the silent prayer of ˋ Hagar? How did God respond? (21:9-20)
c. What might have been the prayer behind the cries of the Children of Israel? (Exodus 1:1-22; 3:7) How did God respond? (3:7-12; 12:13-51)
d. What might have been the prayer behind the tears of the widow of Nain? How did Jesus respond? (Luke 7:11-15)
e. What might have been the prayers behind the cries of the weeping women who followed Jesus? How did Jesus respond? (23:27-31)

Summary Question: Has God ever answered a silent prayer behind a pain in your heart? Share your experience with someone who needs encouragement today.

2. Strange Prayers
Some prayers are not answered because the person praying is a practitioner of evil toward him/herself or toward others.
a. What was the state of Moses when he complained to the Lord? (Numbers 11:10-15, 21) Did God give Moses what he wanted? What was God's response? (11:16-20, 23)

b. What was the state of Israel when it was threatened with an invasion from Assyria? (Isaiah 1:1-10; 16:12) How did God respond to their prayers? (1:15-16) Why? On what conditions would God hear their prayer? (1:18-20)

c. What was the state of the preachers of the Law? How did Jesus respond to the prayers of the teachers of the Law in first century Galilee? (Mark 12:35-40) Why?

d. What was the state of the rich man who died and went to Hades? How did Abraham respond? (Luke 16:19-31)

e. What was the state of the Pharisees when they prayed? How did Jesus respond to their prayer? Why? (18:9-14)

Summary Question: Considering your answers to a-e above, what do these prayers have in common? What can we learn from these stories about prayer?

3. Praying with the Wrong Motives

Some people do not experience their prayers being answered because they pray with the wrong motives.

a. Why was Jeremiah told not to pray for the Israelites around the turn of the sixth century B.C.? (Jeremiah 7:1-4, 16-20; 11:14)

b. What was the state of the hypocrites? How did Jesus respond to their prayers? (Matthew 5:20; 6:5-8)

c. What was the state of the wife of Zebedee? (Matthew 20:20-21) How did Jesus respond to her request? (20:22-28)

d. What was the state of James and John? (Mark 10:35-37) How did Jesus respond to their request? (10:38-45)

e. What is one major reason that God does not grant us some of our requests?
(James 4:1-6) What is the solution to this problem? (4:7-10)

Summary Question: During this upcoming week, ask God to search your heart and reveal whether there are any wrong motives behind your prayers. Based on the insights gained from your answers to a-e above, what changes should you make in your prayer life?

4. Inappropriate Requests

Some prayers are unanswered because God sees the condition of the person praying, who makes an inappropriate request.

a. What was the emotional state of Elijah when he fled to Beersheba? (1 Kings 19:1-5, 10) What did he want? What does his prayer reveal about him? Why was it inappropriate? How did God respond? (19:5-18)

b. What was the state of the people of Judah during a drought around the turn of the sixth century B.C.? (Jeremiah 14:1-6) What was their prayer? (14:7-9) Why was their prayer inappropriate? (14:10-15) How would the Lord respond? (14:15-16)

c. In what state was Habakkuk when he sought the Lord near the end of the seventh century B.C.? (Habakkuk 1:12-17) How did the Lord respond? (2:1-4)

d. What was the state of Peter on the Mount of Transfiguration? (Luke 9:28-33) Why were his statements to Jesus inappropriate? (9:33) How did God respond? (9:34-36)

e. What was the state of the two criminals who were crucified with Jesus? (Mark 15:32; Luke 23:32, 39-43) What was the difference between their prayers? Why did Jesus respond to one and ignore the other?

Summary Question: What are the similarities and differences between the persons praying, examined in a-e above? Can you make any applications from these stories to your personal prayer life?

5. Wrong Attitudes Toward God

Sometimes prayers are not answered because the prayers reflect a wrong attitude toward God.

a. What questions did the people of Israel ask God, during the fifth century B.C., after the temple in Jerusalem had been rebuilt? (Malachi 1:2) What attitude did that prayer reflect? (1:1-3) How did the Lord respond to these people? (1:1-5)

b. What is another question the people of Israel asked God? (1:6) What attitude did that prayer reflect? What was God's response? (1:7-8)

c. What other comments did the Israelites make to God? (1:7, 11-13) What attitude did this reflect? What was God's response? (1:13-14)

d. What is another question the Israelites asked God? (3:6-7) What does the question reflect about the Israelites who asked it? What was God's response? (3:8-12)

e. What is another question the Israelites asked God? (3:13) What does this question reflect about the Israelites? How did God respond? (3:1-5)

Summary Question: Compare and contrast the various attitudes reflected in the questions the Israelites posed to God. How are their questions and attitudes similar to those of people today? What applications from this can you make to your life?

6. Ministry Application

Prepare a series of short, one-paragraph or "good for thought" pieces that could be included in your Sunday Bulletin, based on the insights gained from Exercises #1-5.

7. Personal Application

Read Psalm 139:23-24, and state it to God as prayer. Then listen closely for God's answer.

From the Pastor's Pen

Prayer is not an obligation. Prayer is not a duty. Prayer is not to be feared or a hasty exercise of repeating the same words in a boring conversation with God. Prayer is not an "ought" that makes us feel guilty when we refuse to do it.

Prayer is the excitement of experiencing a loving relationship with the inspiring presence of God. Prayer is our romance with God, our sharing with our Best Friend who is closer than breathing and nearer than hands or feet.

CHAPTER TWELVE

LEARNING TO TALK TO GOD

"Likewise the Spirit also helpeth our infirmities: for we know not what we should pray for as we ought: but the Spirit itself maketh intercession for us with groanings which cannot be uttered" (Romans 8:26, KJV).

"O LORD God of my salvation, I have cried day and night before thee"
(Psalm 88:1, KJV)

INTRODUCTION

God hears our cries and groans as if we were repeating a beautifully worded prayer. This means that the baby Christian who has trouble putting into words her or his deepest feelings is heard by God, as well as those persons who are experienced in uttering beautifully phrased prayers. Praying to God is like learning a new language.

THE LANGUAGE IS LEARNED, NOT CREATED BY THE STUDENT

When you learned to speak English, you moved beyond the crying and moaning stage. You did not create a word. You learned a word and then kept on practicing until you could pronounce the word clearly and distinctly. Your efforts continued until you could speak enough words to express a complete thought. You moved from saying, "Water," to saying, "Want water," to saying, "I want a drink of water, please." So it is when you learn to talk to God. You may babble, "Mercy"; then you progress to saying, "O merciful God, grant Your child mercy this day." God understands your spiritually infantile cries, your preschool spiritual babbles, and your discipleship oriented prayers.

You learn by listening. You learn by repeating again and again what you have heard. You learn by enlarging your vocabulary and by learning the rules of grammar. You learn to pray by listening and by repetition. You learn by enlarging your prayer vocabulary and by learning the grammar of prayer. Listen to the prayers of the Bible. Learn the grammar of prayer from Jesus. Let us repeat in unison the prayer Jesus taught His disciples: "Our Father which art in heaven . . ." (Matthew 6:9).

THE GRAMMAR OF THE TEXT
Let's look at the grammar of the prayer in Psalm 88:1,

"O LORD, the God who saves me, day and night I cry out before you"
(NIV)

The subject is "I."
The action word or verb is "cry."
The adverb that describes how, is "out"— "cry out."
The adverb of time that describes when, is "day and night." This means that I am passionately crying out to God all of the time. It means that I am always in the psychological mood of being in need of God's presence, protection and power. The preposition or connecting word is "before." To "cry out before" is to cry out in the presence of the living God. The word after "cry out before" is the pronoun, "you." A pronoun takes the place of the noun, "God." Here, "you" is a pronoun in the objective case. *God is the object* of our prayers, not our political party, not our purses, not our power and prestige, not peers, not popular personalities—*God is the object* of and for our praying.

Of our praying, means that our prayers are God's possessions, and for our praying, means that God is the purpose to whom we pray. "O LORD, the God who saves" is an adjectival phrase that modifies "God," the objective pronoun. The adjectival phrase explains to us that God is the prayer answering God. The text describes God as "O LORD." The fact that God is LORD means that God is sovereign; that God is powerful; that God gets the job done; that God can be relied upon. The text does not say, "Lord." The text says, "O LORD"! The word "O" is an interjection. An interjection is a word of passion, feeling, and emotion. "O LORD" describes the seriousness and emotional intensity of the person praying. "O LORD" is a serious gesture or exclamation designed to get God's attention. To say, "O LORD" is to say I am for real. I am not praying a formal prayer. I am crying out to You and before You in the state of personal emergency. Bring help yesterday. I don't have time to wait.

"O LORD, the God who saves . . ." "The God who saves" is an adjectival phrase that explains why I cry out to God. It is not a waste of time to pray to the God, because the God saves: The God gets the job done. The article limits what we mean by God. We pray not to a God. We pray to the God.

CONTEMPLATIVE PRAYER

"Who is among you that feareth the LORD . . .
that obeyeth the voice of his servant,
that walketh in darkness, and hath no light? let him trust in the name of
the LORD, and stay upon his God" (Isaiah 50:10, KJV).

"And I will give them an heart to know me,
that I am the LORD:
and they shall be my people,
and I will be their God:
for they shall return unto me with their whole heart"
(Jeremiah 24:7, KJV).

MEDITATION

Meditation is the repetitive invocation of the name of Jesus (Jesus, Jesus, Jesus) in the heart emptied of images and cares.

The aim of meditation is not to arrive at an objective and apparently scientific knowledge about God, but to know Him through the realization that our very being is penetrated with His knowledge and love for us.

Our knowledge of God is paradoxically a knowledge not of Him as the object of our scrutiny, but of ourselves as utterly dependent on His saving and merciful knowledge of us. It is in proportion as we are known to Him that we find our real being and identity in Christ.

We know God in and through ourselves in so far as truth is the source of our being and His merciful love is the very heart of our life and existence. We have no reason for being, except to be loved by Him as our Creator and Redeemer, and to love Him in return. There is no true knowledge of God that does not imply a profound grasp and an intimate personal acceptance of this profound relationship.

The whole purpose of meditation is to deepen the consciousness of this basic relationship of the creature to the Creator and the sinner to his or her Redeemer.

Our meditation should begin with the realization of our nothingness and helplessness in the presence of God.

PRAYER

Prayer means a yearning for the simple presence of God, for a personal understanding of His Word, for knowledge of His will, and for capacity to hear and obey Him.

"May I know You, may I know myself."

We must frankly admit that self-denial and sacrifice are absolutely essential to the life of prayer.

We must control our thoughts and our desires. If we fast, we must make sure we are fasting for the right motives. Prayer and sacrifice work together. Where there is no sacrifice, there will eventually turn out to be no prayer and vice versa.

Prayer can consist partly of psalms and partly of the person's own single and spontaneous words or wordless acts directed at God.

Prayer can be a prayer of silence and simplicity, contemplative and meditative unity, a deep personal integration in an attentive, watchful listening of the heart. It is a wordless and total surrender of the heart in silence.

By prayer of the heart we seek the presence of God Himself in the depths of our being, and we meet Him there by invoking the name of Jesus in faith, wonder and love.

We have to rely on the Holy Spirit, unaffected love, the truth, and the power of God.

If prayer is not itself deeply powerful and pure, filled at all times with the spirit of contemplation, prayer will be more for our own glory and not for the glory of God.

We have to be pure-minded, enlightened, forgiving, and gracious to others; we have to rely on the Holy Spirit, on unaffected love, on the truth of our love, on the truth of our message, and on the power of God. To the right and left we must be armed with innocence:

• now honored; now slighted

• now traduced; now flattered

• they call us deceivers; and we tell the truth

• unknown; and we are freely acknowledged

• dying men and women; and see, we live

• punished; yes, but not doomed to die

• sad men and women; that rejoice continually

• beggars; that bring riches to many

• disinherited; and the world is ours.

(2 Corinthians 6:6-10, paraphrased)

We cannot survive in this paradoxical state without special help from grace and without the ever renewed self-discipline of prayer.

CONCLUSION
We pray to the God, Creator of heaven and earth. We pray to the God who is the sustainer of the universe. We pray to the God who creates, sustains, redeems, heals, cleanses and who chooses us to serve. This God forgives us of our failures and fumblings, and hears us when we pray. This God helps us in our weakness. When we do not know what we ought to pray for, the Holy Spirit intercedes for us with groans that words cannot express.

So pray anyhow. Pray in your weakness. Pray in your doubts, your fears, you sins, your shortcomings. But, pray anyhow. In the morning, pray. In the evening, pray. At midnight, pray. God may not answer you when you want an answer. But hold on. Don't give up hope. The God who answered Jesus three days after the Crucifixion, will resurrect you. Even if you must endure your own betrayal, desertion, and crucifixion, the God who raised Jesus from the dead will resurrect you!

BIBLE STUDY APPLICATION
INSTRUCTIONS: The exercises below provide the opportunity to study more closely the points raised in this chapter.

1. Disposition
The Bible contains important information about the disposition one can adopt when praying.

a. If we expect God to forgive wrongs we have done, what should we do? (Matthew 6:12-14)
b. What is a reason that God grants requests made in Jesus' name? (John 16:23-26)
c. What is an essential frame of mind when we approach God in prayer? (Matthew 21:18-22; Mark 11:22-26)
d. What is one importance of asking for something in Jesus' name? (John 14:13-15)
e. Why can we expect God to give us what we need to carry out our ministries? (John 15:16)

Summary Question: In what ways can insights from these Scriptures improve your prayer life?

2. Praying with and for Others
It is important to pray with and for one another.
a. List nine things for which we should pray for our brothers and sisters in Christ. (Colossians 1:9-14)
b. When, as a group, we approach God in prayer, what should be the content of our prayers? (Ephesians 5:19, 20)
c. Before offering ourselves to God, what should we do? (Matthew 5:21-24)
d. Why should Christians pray together? (Matthew 18:19, 20)
e. What enables Christians to praise God in unity? (Romans 15:5-6)

Summary Question: How can insights from the above questions help your relationship with other Christians?

3. Discipline
Prayer is a discipline, similar to exercise.
a. What enables us to pray in spite of troubles? (Romans 12:12)
b. What enables us not to give up when we encounter adverse circumstances? (Ephesians 6:18, 19)
c. What enables us to be thankful in all circumstances? (1 Thessalonians 5:16-18)
d. What can we learn from Daniel about prayer? (Daniel 6:6-26; 10)
e. What is a major outcome of a disciplined prayer life? (Psalm 23)

Summary Question: How can insights from the above Scriptures improve your personal prayer life?

4. The Role of the Holy Spirit in Prayer

The Holy Spirit plays an important role in our communications with God.

a. What enables us to call God our Father (and/or Mother)? (Romans 8:15)

b. Why does the Holy Spirit groan with and in us? (8:23)

c. What happens when our pain is so great that we cannot express it in words to God? (8:26-27)

d. How do we experience the peace of God in spite of difficult challenges? (Philippians 4:6-7)

e. Wha† is one form that the Holy Spirit takes? (John 14:27)

Summary Question: How can insights from the above Scriptures affect the way you approach God in prayer?

5. The Power of Prayer

Prayer changes things!

a. What is one basis for believing that prayer changes things? (Matthew 7:7-11)

b. What is a basis for believing that believers can endure hardships? (2 Thessalonians 3:1-5)

c. What is the basis for believing that you will have the wisdom to handle difficult situations? (James 1:5-8)

d. What is another basis for believing that prayer changes things? (1:17-18)

e. Is God still in the healing business? (5:13-18)

Summary Question: How can insights gained from the above Scriptures improve your prayer life?

6. Ministry Application

Propose to your pastor the idea of adding a devotional period to the church business meeting(s) that you attend, if you do not already have one. In the devotional period, add a time of silent reflection and meditation. Then take note of the difference it makes in the tone of the meeting.

7. Personal Application

What is a major point made by Dr. Smith in this chapter that applies to your prayer life? How do you intend to apply it?

ENDNOTES

INTRODUCTION

[1] Rayford Logan and Michael Winston, *Dictionary of American Negro Biography* (New York: W.W. Norton and Company, 1982), p. 12.

[2] Sharon Harley, *The Timetable of African American History* (New York: A Touchstone Book, 1995), pp. 32-34.

[3] Harley, *Timetable of African American History*, p. 38.

[4] Harley, pp. 42, 44 and William Foster, *The Negro People* (New York: International Publishers, 1954), p. 45.

[5] Harley, p. 48.

[6] Harley, p. 48.

[7] Harley, p. 46.

[8] Harley, p. 46.

[9] Harley, p. 46.

[10] Harley, p. 50.

[11] Harley, p. 52.

[12] Harley, p. 52.

[13] Harley, p. 52.

[14] Harley, p. 44.

[15] Harley, p. 56.

[16] Harley, p. 56.

[17] James Melvin Washington, *Conversations with God: Two Centuries of Prayers of African Americans* (New York: HarperPerennial, 1994), p. 8.

[18] Jacquelline Bernard, *Journey Toward Freedom* (New York: Dell, 1967), pp. 64-66.

[19] Bernard, p. 64.

[20] Logan and Winston, pp. 604-605.

[21] Washington, p. 55.

[22] Michael Harris, *The Rise of Gospel Blues* (New York: Oxford University Press, 1992), p. 218.

[23] Harris, p. 217.

[24] Harris, pp. 209-221.

[25] Washington, p. 154.

CHAPTER ONE
[1] John 3:30, paraphrased.

[2] See Psalm 84:10.

[3] Frederick Ward Kates, *A Moment Between Two Eternities* (New York, Evanston, and London: Harper Chapel Books, 1965), p. 1.

[4] *Ibid.*

[5] Arnold J. Toynbee, *A Study Of History,* Volume X, 1954, p. 128. (Oxford University, Oxford, England)

CHAPTER TWO
[1] Hardy R. Denham, Jr., *Living Toward a Vision* (Nashville: Broadman Press, 1980), pp. 9-10.

[2] *Ibid.*

[3] *Ibid.*

[4] *Ibid.*

CHAPTER THREE
[1] Eberhard Bethge (ed.), *Letters and Papers from Prison* (New York: MacMillan, 1971), p. 139.

[2] Mrs. Charles E. Cowan, *Streams in the Desert* (Grand Rapids: Zondervan Publishing House, 1925), p. 167.

[3] *Ibid.*, pp. 386-387.

CHAPTER FOUR
[1] James Mudge (ed.), *Formal Prayer Poems with Power* (Nashville: Abingdon Cokesbury Press, 1907), p. 134. This is an anonymous prayer.

[2] Frederick Ward Kates, *A Moment Between Two Eternities* (New York, Evanston and London: Harper Chapel Books, 1965), p. 1.

[3] *Ibid.*

CHAPTER FIVE
[1] Anonymous

CHAPTER SIX
[1] Donald G. Bloesch, *The Struggle of Prayer* (Colorado Springs: Helmers and Howard, 1988), p. 78.

CHAPTER SEVEN
[1] Dwight Hopkins, *Shoes That Fit Our Feet* (Maryknoll, New York: Orbis Books, 1993), p. 170.

CHAPTER EIGHT
[1] Jessie Jai McNeal, *As Thy Days So Thy Strength* (Grand Rapids: Eerdmans Publishing Company, 1960), p. 73.

[2] Walter McCray, *The Black Presence in the Bible* (Chicago: Black Light Fellowship, 1990), p. 31.

[3] Anthony T. Evans, *Are Blacks Spiritually Inferior to Whites?* (Wenonah: Renaissance Productions, 1992), pp. 59-62.

[4] E. Bolaji Idowu, *Olïd£marä, God in Yoruba Belief* (London: Longmans, 1962), p. 131.

[5] Evans, p. 63.

[6] Bishop W. J. Gaines, D.D., *The United Negro: His Problems and His Progress, Containing the Addresses and Proceedings of the Negro Young People's Christian and Educational Congress, Held August 6-11, 1902* (Atlanta: D.E. Luther Publishing, 1902), pp. 102-105.

[7] "Walk with Me," Negro Spiritual, *The New National Baptist Hymnal*, Second

Edition (Nashville: National Baptist Publishing Board), p. 503.

CHAPTER NINE
[1] *Christian Clippings,* P.O. Box 7077 (Wesley Chapel, 1993), p. 1. Anonymous author.

[2] Cleavant Derricks, "Just a Little Talk with Jesus," *The Progressive National Baptist Hymnal,* Progressive National Baptist Convention, Inc. Publishing Board (Washington, 1982) p.298.

CHAPTER TEN
[1] Cecil Osborne, *The Art of Understanding Yourself* (Grand Rapids: Zondervan Publishing Company, 1956), p. 103.

[2] Cain Hope Felder, *Troubling Biblical Waters: Race, Class and Family* (Maryknoll: Orbis Books, 1989), p.15.

[3] Cheikh Anta Diop, *The African Origins of Civilization: Myth or Reality?* (Westport: Lawrence Hill, 1987), pp.1-20.

[4] Charles Copher's, "The Black Man in the Biblical World" Journal of I.T.C., Volume 1, No. 2 (Spring, 1994), pp. 7-16.

CHAPTER ELEVEN
[1] The scripture is from the King James Version of the Bible Luke 18:11-12.

[2] Charlotte Elliott, "Just As I Am", *The New Progressive Baptist Hymnal,* Progressive National Baptist Convention, Inc. Publishing Board (Washington, 1982), p.145.

BIBLIOGRAPHY

Adetunji, J.A. "Church-based Obstetric Care in a Yoruba Community, Nigeria," *Social Science and Medicine Volume,* 35, No. 9, November, 1992, pp. 1171-8.

Adney, Carol. *This Morning with God.* Downer's Grove: InterVarsity Press, 1978.

Alexander, John. *This Morning with God.* Downer's Grove: InterVarsity Press, 1980.

Allen, Earl. *Prayers That Changed History.* Nashville: Broadman Press, 1977.

Appleton, George. *The Oxford Book of Prayer.* New York: Oxford University Press, 1992.

Arinero, J.G., translated by Kathleen Pond. *Stages in Prayer.* London: Blackfriars, 1957.

Ash, J. "Prayer on Night Duty," *Christian Nurse International,* Volume 9, No. 3, 1993, pp. 9-10.

Au, Wilkie S.J. *By Way of the Heart: Toward a Holistic Christian Spirituality.* New York: Paulist Press, 1989.

Bacon, J. "Healing Prayer: The Risks and Rewards," *Journal of Christian Nursing,* Vol. 12, No. 1, Winter, 1995, pp. 14-17.

Baillie, John. *A Diary of Private Prayer.* New York: Charles Scribner's Sons, 1949.

Balentine, Samuel E. *Prayer in the Hebrew Bible.* Minneapolis: Fortress Press, 1993.

Banks, Walter L. *How to Pray and Communicate with God.* Chicago: Urban Ministries, Inc., 1988.

Barth, Karl. *Prayer and Preaching.* Naperville, IL: SCM Book Club, 1964.

Becker, Nancy. "Teaching People to Pray," *Leadership,* Volume 5, No. 1, Winter, 1984, pp. 106-108.

Bishop, Shelton Hale. *The Wonder of Prayer.* Greenwich: Seabury Press, 1959.

Blackwood, Andrew J. *Prayers for All Occasions.* Grand Rapids: Baker Book House, 1990.

Bloesch, Donald. *The Struggle of Prayer.* San Francisco: Harper & Row, 1980.

Bloom, Anthony. *Beginning to Pray.* New York: Paulist Press, 1970.

Boesak, Allan and Charles Villa-Vicencio. *When Prayer Makes News.* Philadelphia: Westminister Press, 1986.

Boulding, Maria. *Prayer: Our Journey Home.* Ann Arbor: Servant Books, 1979.

Bowyer, O. Richard, Betty L. Hart, and Charlotte A. Meade. *Prayer in the Black Tradition.* Nashville: Upper Room, 1986.

Brokhoff, John R. *Pray Like Jesus.* Lima, OH: CSS Publishing House, 1994.

Byrd, R.C. and J. Sherrill. "The Therapeutic Effects of Intercessory Prayer,"

Journal of Christian Nursing, Volume 12, No. 1, Winter, 1995, pp. 21-23.

Carney, Gladion and William Long. *Longing for God*. Downers Grove: InterVarsity Press, 1993.

Carroll, S. "Spirituality and Purpose in Life in Alcoholism Recovery," *Journal of Studies on Alcohol*, Volume 54, No. 3, May, 1993, pp. 297-301.

Carson, V.B. "Prayer, Meditation, Exercise and Special Diets: Behaviors of the Hardy Person with HIV/AIDS," *Journal of the Association of Nurses in AIDS Care*, Vol. 4, No. 3, July-September, 1993, pp. 18-28.

Carter, Harold. *The Prayer Tradition of Black People*. Valley Forge: Judson Press, 1976.

Chadwick, Samuel. *The Path of Prayer*. London: Hodder and Stoughton, 1931.

Clark, Kelly James. *Quiet Times for Christian Growth*. Downer's Grove: InterVarsity Press, 1976.

Cornelison, A.H. "Prayer Is a Nursing Intervention," *American Journal of Nursing*, Vol. 93, No. 9, September, 1993, p. 14.

Cooper, Darien B. *The Beauty of Beholding God*. Wheaton: Victor Books, 1982.

Costen, Melva Wilson. *African American Christian Worship*. Nashville: Abingdon Press, 1993.

Davis, T. "The Research Evidence on the Power of Prayer and Healing," *Canadian Journal of Cardiovascular Nursing*, Volume 5, No. 2, 1994, pp. 34-6.

Doughty, W.L., ed. *The Prayers of Susanna Wesley*. Grand Rapids: Zondervan Publishing House, 1984.

Douglas, James W. *Resistance and Contemplation: The Way of Liberation*. New York: Dell, 1972.

Ellison, C.G. "Race, Religious Involvement and Depressive Symptomatology in a Southeastern United States Community," *Social Science and Medicine*, Vol. 40, No. 11, June, 1995, pp. 1561-72.

Finney, Charles G. *Principles of Prayer*. Minneapolis: Bethany House Publishers, 1980.

Fish, S. "Can Research Prove that God Answers Prayer?" *Journal of Christian Nursing*, Volume 12, Winter, 1995, pp. 24-27.

Forbes, James. *The Holy Spirit and Preaching*. Nashville: Abingdon Press, 1989.

Foster, Richard J. *Prayer*. San Francisco: Harper and Row Publishers, 1992.

Gayles, Gloria Wade. *My Soul Is a Witness: African American Women's Spirituality*. Boston: Beacon Press, 1995.

——————————.*Pushed Back to Strength: A Black Woman's Journey Home*. Boston: Beacon Press, 1992.

Goodrich, C.A. *Bible History of Prayer*. London: Case, Tiffany, Hartford, 1850.

Goodwin, Bennie E. *Pray Right, Live Right*. Downer's Grove: InterVarsity Press, 1979.

Gould, D., R.C. Eklund and S.A. Jackson. "Coping Strategies Used by U.S. Olympic Wrestlers," *Research Quarterly for Exercise and Sport*, Volume 64,

No. 1, March, 1993, pp. 83-93.

Griffiths, Michael. *The Example of Jesus,* Downer's Grove: InterVarsity Press, 1985.

Hall, Thelma. *Too Deep for Words.* New York: Paulist Press, 1988.

Hancock, "Prayer Beyond the Ordinary," *Journal of Christian Nursing,* Vol. 10, No. 2, Spring, 1993, pp.16-19.

Harkness, Georgia. *A Devotional Treasury from the Early Church.* Nashville and New York: Abingdon Press, 1968.

Hill, H.M., S. R. Hawkins, M. Raposo, and P. Carr. "Relationship Between Multiple Exposures to Violence and Coping Strategies Among African-American Mothers," *Violence and Victims,* Vol. 10, No. 1, Spring, 1995, pp. 55-71.

Hollings, M. and E. Gulick, eds. *The One Who Listens: A Book of Prayer.* New York: Morehouse-Barlow, 1971.

Hubbard, David Allen. *The Practice of Prayer.* Downer's Grove: InterVarsity Press, 1983.

Huggett, Joyce. *The Joy of Listening to God.* Downer's Grove: InterVarsity Press, 1986.

Hummel, Charles. *Filled with the Spirit.* Downer's Grove: InterVarsity Press, 1981.

Hunter, W. Bingham. *The God Who Hears.* Downer's Grove: InterVarsity Press, 1981.

Hurston, Zora Neale. *Moses, Man of the Mountain.* Urbana and Chicago: University of Illinois Press, 1984.

InterVarsity Press. *First Mornings with God.* Downer's Grove: InterVarsity Press, 1986.

Johnson, Ben Campbell. *Pastoral Spirituality.* Philadelphia: Westminster Press, 1988.

Kaye, J. and Robinson, K.M. "Spirituality Among Caregivers," *Image: the Journal of Nursing Scholarship,* Volume 26, No. 3, Fall, 1994, pp. 218-21.

Klos, Sarah. *Prayers Alone/Together.* Philadelphia: Fortress Press, 1970.

Kunz, Maryland. *Patterns for Living with God.* Downer's Grove: InterVarsity Press, 1961.

LaVerdiere, Eugene. *When We Pray: Meditation on the Lord's Prayer.* Notre Dame, IN: Ave Maria Press, 1983.

Levin, J.S., J. S. Lyons and D.B. Larson, "Prayer and Health During Pregnancy: Findings from the Galveston Low Birthweight Survey," *Southern Medical Journal,* Volume 86, No. 9, September, 1993, pp. 1022-7.

Lockyer, Herbert. *All the Prayers of the Bible.* Grand Rapids: Zondervan Publishing House, 1959.

Lofton, Fred. *A Crying Shepherd.* Winter Park, FL: 4 G Publishers, 1993.

————————————.*Teach Us to Pray: The Disciples' Request Cast Anew.* Elgin: Progressive National Baptist Convention.

Marwick, C. "Should Physicians Prescribe Prayer for Health? Spiritual Aspects of Well-Being Considered," *Journal of the American Medical Association*, Volume 273, No. 20, May 24-31, 1995, pp. 1561-2.

Mason, C.H., "Prayer as a Nursing Intervention," *Journal of Christian Living*, Vol. 12, No. 1, Winter, 1995, pp. 4-8.

Maynard, Robert C., with Dori Maynard. *Letters to My Children*. Kansas City, MO: Universal Press Syndicate Company, 1995.

Mbiti, John. *The Prayers of African Religion*. Maryknoll: Orbis Books, 1975.

McClendon, James William Jr. *Biography as Theology: How Life Stories Can Remake Today's Theology*. Nashville: Abingdon Press, 1974.

McEachern, Alton. *A Pattern for Prayer*. Brentwood: J.M. Productions, 1982.

McNeil, Jesse Jai. *As Thy Days So Thy Strength*. Grand Rapids: William B. Eerdmans, 1960.

Merton, Thomas. *Contemplative Prayer*. Garden City, NY: Doubleday, 1971.

Micklenn, Carlyl and Roger Tomes. *As Good as Your Word: A Third Book of Contemporary Prayers*. Grand Rapids: Eerdmans Publishing Company, 1975.

Miller, Craig Kennett. *Baby Boomer Spirituality: Ten Essential Values of a Generation*. Nashville: Discipleship Resources, 1992.

Miller, Herb. *Connecting with God*. Nashville: Abingdon Press, 1994.

Miller, Samuel H. *Man, The Believer*. Nashville and New York: Abingdon Pess, 1968.

Neufelder, Jerome M. and Mary C. Coelho. *Writings on Spiritual Direction by Great Christian Masters*. New York: Seabury Press, 1982.

Niebuhr, Reinhold, and Ursula M. Niebuhr, eds. *Justice and Mercy*. New York, San Francisco: Harper and Row, 1974.

Paris, Peter. *The Spirituality of African People*. Minneapolis: Fortress Press, 1995.

Phillips, George W. *The Hour of Prayer*. Oakland: Radio Church Office, Volume I, K.T.A.B., 1929.

——————————. *The Hour of Prayer*. Oakland: Radio Church Office Volume II, 1929.

——————————. *The Hour of Prayer*. Oakland: Radio Church Office Volume III, 1931.

Postema, Don. *Space for God: The Study and Practice of Prayer and Spirituality*. Grand Rapids: Bible Way, 1983.

Sanders, J. Oswald. *Spiritual Leadership*. Chicago: Moody Press, 1967, 1980.

Scharfe, G., J. "One Step On, Healing Prayer in a Secular Setting?" *Christian Nurse International*, Vol. 9, No. 3, 1993, pp. 6-8.

Schmitz, Charles H. *Windows Toward God*. Nashville: Abingdon-Cokesbury Press, 1950.

Shelly, J.A. "Is Prayer Unprofessional?" *Journal of Christian Nursing*, Vol. 12, No. 1, Winter, 1995, p. 3.

Shuler, P.A., L. Gelberg, and M. Brown. "The Effects of Spiritual/Religious

Practices on Psychological Well-Being Among Inner-City Homeless Women," *Nurse Practitioner Forum,* Volume 5, No. 2, June, 1994, pp. 106-13.

Smith, J. Alfred Sr. *Making Sense of Suffering: A Message to Job's Children.* Elgin: Progressive National Baptist Convention, 1988.

——————. *The Overflowing Heart.* Nashville: Broadman Press, 1987.

——————. *A Prayer Wheel Turning: Selected Pastoral Prayers.* Morristown: Aaron Press, 1989.

Sorter, Aylward. *Prayer in the Religious Traditions of Africa.* New York: Oxford University Press, 1975.

Stern, R.C., E.R. Canda, and C.F. Doershuk. "Use of Non-Medical Treatment by Cystic Fibrosis Patients," *Journal of Adolescent Health,* Volume 13, No. 7, November, 1992, pp. 612-4.

Strauss, Lehman. *Sense and Nonsense About Prayer.* Chicago: Moody Press, 1974.

Thomas, G. Ernest. *Spiritual Life in the New Testament.* Fleming H. Revell Company.

Thurman, Howard. *The Centering Moment.* Richmond: Friends United Press, 1969.

——————. *The Creative Encounter: An Interpretation of Religion and the Social Witness.* Richmond: Friends United Press, 1954.

——————. *Disciplines of the Spirit.* New York, Evanston, and London: Harper and Row, 1963.

——————. *Jesus and the Disinherited.* Nashville: Abingdon Press, 1949.

——————. *The Growing Edge.* Richmond: Friends United Press, 1956.

——————. *The Inward Journey.* Richmond: Friends United Press, 1961.

——————. *The Luminous Darkness.* New York, Evanston, and London: Harper and Row, 1965.

——————. *The Negro Speaks of Life and Death.* New York: Harper and Row, 1947.

——————. *The Search for Common Ground.* New York, Evanston, San Francisco, London: Harper and Row, 1971.

——————. *Temptations of Jesus.* Richmond: Friends United Press, 1962.

Thurston, Bonnie. *Spiritual Life in the Early Church: The Witness of Acts and Ephesians.* Minneapolis: Fortress Press, 1993.

Tutu, Desmond. *An African Prayer Book.* New York, London, Toronto: Doubleday, 1995.

Tyms, James D. *Spiritual Values in the Black Poet.* Washington, DC: University Press of America, 1979.

Van Kaam, Adrian. *Spirituality and the Gentle Life.* Denville: Dimension

Books, Inc., 1974.

Vardey, Lucinda. *Mother Theresa: A Simple Path.* New York: Ballantine Books, 1995.

Walker, Wyatt Tee. *The Soul of Black Worship: A Trilogy—Preaching, Praying, Singing.* New York: Martin Luther King, Jr. Fellows Press, 1984.

Washington, James Melvin *Conversations with God.* New York: HarperPerennial, 1994.

White, John. *Daring to Draw Near.* Downer's Grove: InterVarsity Press, 1977.

Wicks, Robert J. *Touching the Holy.* Notre Dame: Ave Maria Press, 1992.

Wiersbe, Warren. *Listen, Jesus Is Praying.* Wheaton: Tyndale Publishers, Inc., 1982.

Wimberly, Edward P. *Prayer in Pastoral Counseling.* Louisville: Westminster Press, 1990.

Wirth, D. P. and J. R. Cram. "The Psychophysiology of Non-Traditional Prayer," *International Journal of Psychosomatics,* Volume 41, No. 1-4, 1994, pp. 68-75.

Wirth, D.P. and M. J. Barrett. "Complimentary Healing Therapies," *International Journal of Psychosomatics,* Volume 41, No. 1-4, 1994, pp. 61-7.

BIOGRAPHY

Dr. J. Alfred Smith, Sr. is the Senior Pastor of Allen Temple Baptist Church. He is Professor of Christian Ministry at the American Baptist Seminary of the West and the Graduate Theological Union of Berkeley. He is currently Visiting Professor at Fuller Theological Seminary. He has served as Acting Dean of the American Baptist Seminary of the West, and as Area Representative for the American Baptist Churches of the West.

He has served as Visiting Professor at numerous seminaries across the country, including the Southern Baptist Theological Seminary, Louisville, Kentucky, and Harvard University School of Divinity. He has also been guest lecturer for the Hoskins Lectures on Ministry at the School of Divinity at Yale University, and guest lecturer at the School of Divinity at Duke University. Dr. Smith has been Distinguished Pastor in Residence at the School of Divinity of Howard University.

Dr. Smith is the Past President of the American Baptist Churches of the West and the Progressive National Baptist Convention.

Dr. Smith is the Founding Chairperson of the Bay Area Black United Fund, a member of the Advisory Boards of the School of Divinity of Howard University and the United Theological Seminary. He is also a member of the University of California, Berkeley Community Advisory Board, the California State Legislator's Commission on the African American Male, a member of the Advisory Board of the National Conference of Black Seminarians, and a member of the Executive Board of the National Council of Churches.

Dr. Smith has traveled extensively to speak at churches, universities, and seminaries nationwide. He addressed the Baptist World Alliance when the body convened in Toronto, Canada, and in Seoul, Korea. He served as preacher for the 1991 Bermuda Bible Conference. He has spoken in West Africa, Jerusalem, Sweden, Denmark, Mexico, Canada, Switzerland, and the Virgin Islands. In April of 1989, Dr. Smith addressed the United Nations on apartheid in South Africa and the anti-apartheid efforts of African American churches. In February, 1988 Dr. Smith led a delegation from the U.S. on a fact-finding mission to Sierra Leone, where he and others have established a Baptist Mission.

Dr. Smith is the author of 16 books which are used by seminaries, Bible students, teachers, and scholars worldwide. Recent publications include: *Giving to a Giving God, Basic Bible Sermons,* a chapter in *From Prison Cell to Church Pew,* and a sermon in *Best Sermons for 1993.* He is a contributing author of Holman Bible Publisher's *The Study Bible.* Books on Dr. Smith and Allen Temple include *Guidelines for Effective Urban Ministry. Preaching as a Social Act* discusses Dr. Smith's personal theology.

The work of Allen Temple Baptist Church and Dr. Smith have been featured in numerous media, including NBC's "Today Show," CNN, *Christianity Today, Ebony* Magazine, *The Oakland Tribune, The San Francisco Chronicle, The Los Angeles Times, The San Jose Mercury News,* and *The American Baptist* Magazine. A videotape, available through Allen Temple Baptist Church, titled "Caring and Sharing," has been produced highlighting some of the Allen Temple ministries.

Dr. Smith has earned over 125 awards, including those from Stanford University, the Martin Luther King International Chapel of Morehouse College, the National Council of Negro Women, Alpha Phi Alpha, the Bay Area Free South Africa Movement, the U.S. Congress, and AFRICA. He has been elevated to the 33rd Degree of Prince Hall Free and Accepted Masons. In November, 1993 Dr. Smith was named by *Ebony* Magazine as one of America's 15 greatest African American preachers. In 1994, *The Oakland Tribune* named him as the 1994 Outstanding Citizen of the Year. He has received honorary doctorates from Western Baptist College and Inter-Baptist Theological Center. In 1990, Dr. Smith was awarded an Honorary Doctor of Humane Letters from the American Baptist Seminary of the West.

A native of Kansas City, Missouri, Dr. Smith is married to JoAnna Goodwin Smith. He has been a licensed minister since 1948 and an ordained minister since 1951. He earned his Doctor of Ministry from Golden Gate Seminary, his Master of Theology in American Church History from American Baptist Seminary of the West, his Master of Theology in Church and Community and Bachelor of Divinity, both from Missouri School of Religion, and his Bachelor of Science from Western Baptist College. Under his leadership, Allen Temple Baptist Church has grown from fewer than 1,000 members in 1970, to over 4,000 members. As Senior Pastor, Dr. Smith administers over 25 community- and family-oriented programs and services of the church.

THE UMI
LEADERSHIP TRAINING SERIES

How to Pray & Communicate With God
Walter L. Banks

How to Help Hurting People
Dr. Colleen Birchett

Biblical Strategies for a Community in Crisis
Dr. Colleen Birchett

Ordinary People Can Do the Extraordinary
Dr. Bennie Goodwin

How to Equip the African American Family
Drs. George and Yvonne Abatso

How I Got Over
Dr. Colleen Birchett

Africans Who Shaped Our Faith
Dr. Jeremiah A. Wright, Jr.

Seeing With the Heart
Rev. Dr. Johnnie W. Skinner, Sr.

For more information, call 1.800.860.8642